EFFECTIVE MEETINGS

GREAT RESULTS. LESS PAIN. EVERY TIME.

CHRIS FENNING

Effective Meetings: Great Results. Less Pain. Every Time.

Copyright © 2025 by Chris Fenning, Alignment Group Ltd
For more about this author please visit www.chrisfenning.com

For permission requests, bulk orders, and other enquiries, write to:

Alignment Group Ltd,
20-22 Wenlock Road, London, N1 7GU, United Kingdom
www.chrisfenning.com

eBook ISBN: 978-1-916818-11-8
Paperback ISBN: 978-1-916818-09-5
Hardcover ISBN: 978-1-916818-10-1
Audiobook ISBN: 978-1-916818-12-5

Editing by The Pro Book Editor

This book is dedicated to you.
Why? Because you are trying to make your
meetings better and that is a noble thing.

Other books by Chris Fenning

The First Minute
The First Minute Workbook
Effective Emails
39 Ways to Make Training Stick

FREE RESOURCES KIT

Get a free resource kit packed with assessments, guides, activities, templates, and examples. It will help you apply what you learn in this book to the meetings you have every week at work.

https://chrisfenning.com/resources/

TABLE OF CONTENTS

INTRODUCTION

Imagine a world where you have fewer meetings and those meetings are a productive use of everyone's time. Wouldn't that be nice?! That's what this book is all about.

Bad meetings happen far too often, and they suck. I'm not saying *all* meetings are bad, but a lot are.

In a recent survey of 1244 workers, 45 percent of respondents said work meetings actually make them *less* productive in their jobs.[1] Considering the average worker spends five hours per week in meetings[2] and managers spend more than eleven hours, that's a lot of lost productivity. And let's not forget the cost. If you want to know where a good amount of company budgets are wasted, add up the hourly rate of everyone in a meeting and compare it to the value of what is produced.

Solving, or even better, *avoiding* these problems is why I wrote this book. Every page has simple habits, methods, and frameworks you can use to get what you actually need from meetings. And I don't just mean from the ones you lead. These methods help when you are a participant in someone else's meeting too. Some only take a few seconds but can make a big difference.

---

1 "The State of Meetings." https://calendly.com/resources/guides/2024-state-of-meetings-report
2 https://fellow.app/resources/state-of-meetings-2024

Over the course of my twenty-five-year career I've experienced a lot of meetings. And I mean a *lot*. I've led or attended more than 15,000 of them. Roughly half of those happened during an eight-year period where I averaged 25 meetings per week for 48 weeks of the year. Yes, that's a stupidly high number.

What might surprise you is the feedback I got about the meetings I led. Some people actually liked them. Not all of them and definitely not those at the beginning of my career, or even the ones in the middle, but toward the end, *something changed*. Attendance was high, the feedback was good, and most importantly, the meetings usually achieved what was intended. What I learned about running great meetings to achieve that track record is in this book.

There are many books you can buy about how to run meetings. Some go deep into the psychology of team cohesion, others focus on solving problems during meetings, or handling conflict. What was missing is a short, simple book that can quickly solve the majority of meeting problems. So, I wrote this book.

If you use this book, you will learn the simple habits that make meetings more productive, less painful, and much more likely to produce the output you need. You'll get more done with fewer people. There's even a chance those people will appreciate being involved. Imagine that, people actually feeling glad they were in a meeting!

That's quite a large promise to make, so to cover my you-know-what, I'm going to ask you a question. Do all the meetings you lead and attend produce what they need to quickly and efficiently? If your answer is YES, great! You can give this book to a friend or colleague and go back to having awesome meetings. But if your answer is NO, as I suspect it might be, turn the page and discover just how easy it can be to run an effective meeting.

WHAT ABOUT AI?

AI is everywhere right now, so it's natural to wonder if it can help fix meetings. The short answer? Not really. At least, not the parts that matter most.

AI tools can absolutely support your meetings—especially virtual ones. They can take notes, generate summaries, and even nudge you if you're monologuing too much (thank you, Yoodli). That's useful, no doubt. But AI can't tell you the real purpose of your meeting. It won't decide what the output should be. It doesn't know who actually needs to be in the room. And it won't speak up when the conversation starts drifting off track. Those things still require human judgment.

Also, when it comes to in-person meetings, the tech struggles even more. Most AI tools rely on clean audio input—something a single speakerphone in a big glass meeting room isn't exactly known for. Unless your office has podcast-level sound quality, don't expect miracles.

So yes, AI can help with the admin and some nudges, and I've mentioned a few useful tools throughout this book. But the real gains come from doing the things covered in these pages—things only people can do. Set a clear purpose. Define the output. Invite the right people. Keep the discussion focused. These are still human jobs.

For now, at least.

HOW TO USE THIS BOOK

Each chapter in this book covers a different part of a meeting. The first chapter asks, "Do you really need this meeting?" Then each following chapter covers the five stages that make a great meeting: before, start, during, end, and after. The diagram below shows the key activities in each stage.

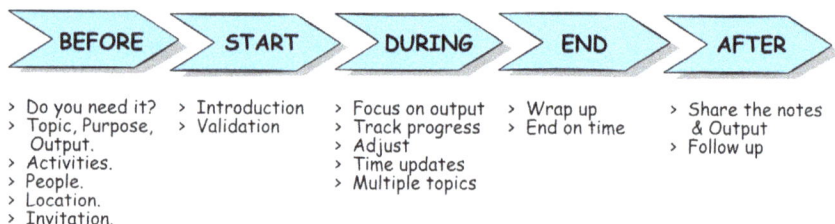

BEFORE	START	DURING	END	AFTER
> Do you need it? > Topic, Purpose, Output. > Activities. > People. > Location. > Invitation.	> Introduction > Validation	> Focus on output > Track progress > Adjust > Time updates > Multiple topics	> Wrap up > End on time	> Share the notes & Output > Follow up

If you're thinking, *I don't have time to do all that for every meeting*, you're not alone. Almost everyone I've taught had the same initial reaction. But before you throw this book aside and go back to running your meetings the way you always have, here are a few reasons why the number of elements in that image isn't as big as it seems.

» Many of them are fast. Some, like picking a location, only take a few seconds to complete.

» You don't do all the steps at the same time. Planning, running, and following up on a meeting happens over a period of time, sometimes spanning days or weeks.

» You're doing many of these things already, unless you're reading this before running your very first meeting! This does not show seventeen new things to add to your already busy workday.

» It's always worth a little extra time on the front end to save a whole lot of time on the backend and the savings add up every time you have a meeting. Just think of what your time investment now could save you over the days, weeks, months, years ahead.

If seventeen still feels like too many, try this—choose which ones to cut from the list. What would happen if you didn't pick the right people or didn't write a clear invitation? Would you choose not to track progress against time? What about finishing on time, can we drop that one?

Every one of these seventeen activities is important to ensure a meeting is productive and efficient. The time and stress they save you during and after the meeting will more than make up for any extra planning time you put in.

The chapters start with short stories real people have shared about bad meetings followed by solutions to help you avoid the same issues in your own meetings. Each chapter ends with an activity or assessment to help you practice and apply what you've learned.

Throughout the book you'll also find advice for when you are trapped in a bad meeting but not leading it, including specific phrases you can use to try and make the meeting pain go away.

You can read this book cover to cover in less than two hours. It'll take a little longer if you do the activities as you go along. Alternatively, if you're struggling with a specific part of a meeting, then jump to the relevant chapter and get the help you want.

When you're done reading and doing the activities, I suggest keeping a copy handy to use as a quick reference. When things are moving fast and you have twenty-three meetings[3] scheduled for next Monday, it will remind you of the simplest ways to make those meetings better.

There is one more way you can use this book to make your workday better: Give it to someone who needs it. Someone whose meetings are so bad that you shudder when you see an invitation from them. Slip a copy onto their desk, mail it to them anonymously, or, if you are feeling bold, place it firmly in their hand, look them in the eye, and say, "You're welcome!"

---

3 - I wish this was a joke, but alas, on one particularly long day I was invited to twenty-three different meetings.

WAIT!!!

DO YOU REALLY NEED THIS MEETING?

"Uurgh! That meeting should have been an email."

DO YOU REALLY NEED THIS MEETING?

Let's face it, some meetings should never have happened. You've probably been in one and thought, "Why am I here?" The truth is, many meetings are just filling up your calendar without a good reason. The problem? The person setting them up didn't stop to consider if a meeting was even necessary.

Somewhere along the way, meetings became the go-to solution for everything. Got a problem? Have a meeting. Need to share an update? Schedule a meeting. Want to catch up with someone? Yep, you guessed it—set up a meeting. But here's the thing: meetings don't always get stuff done. In fact, they can often be a waste of time.

So before you even think about hitting that schedule button in your calendar, let's make sure you actually need a meeting in the first place.

Here are three questions to use as a quick reality check:

1. Do you know what you want to achieve?

2. Do you really need other people's input?

3. Does this need to be a real-time conversation?

If you're shaking your head "no" to any of these, guess what? You don't need a meeting. If you're nodding "yes" to all three, then ask yourself one more thing:

» Can you accomplish the same thing with a phone call, an email, or a quick chat online? If so, skip the meeting.

But if, after all that, you're still convinced that a meeting is the way to go, then great—you're ready to start planning a great meeting.

BE CAREFUL WITH "INFO-ONLY" MEETINGS

If your only goal is to share information, think carefully about whether you need to call a meeting.

If you want people to *do* something with that information—like plan, decide, or create—then having a meeting makes sense. On the other hand, if you just want to deliver information in a one-way flow from you to the audience, a meeting might not be needed, or valuable for the participants. There's a reason the phrase, "That meeting could have been an email" exists. If you just need to pass on info consider if you can send it in an email, in a video, or a in document that people can check out on their own time.

A common argument for info-only meetings is, "They help with employee engagement." I don't agree. No one is engaged when they are forced to sit and listen to someone deliver lists of facts. The word engagement means actively participating or taking part. That's not a passive thing. If your purpose is to engage the audience, think about how to make the session interactive so that people are literally engaging and not just receiving.

EXCEPTIONS TO THE RULES

As you might expect, there are exceptions to this rule. Despite my dislike of one-way info-dump meetings, there are some occasions where delivering information is valuable.

» **Crisis, or Significant Situations:** If something impactful is happening and affects many people, it can help to gather those people together to share information. This ensures everyone hears the same message at the same time and can prevent rumors and misinformation (e.g., staff cuts, something unexpected in the press, and significant celebrations).

» **Town-Hall Business Meetings Such as Quarterly and Annual Updates:** These are okay if the information being shared is valuable to the employees or if there is a need for everyone to hear a message at the same time. But, if the only purpose is for the CFO to read from the financial statement that's not a valuable use of time.

» **When Your Boss Insists on Verbal Updates:** If your boss won't read the weekly report they make you create, and they insist on in-person status updates, keep the number of invitees as small as possible. Try to schedule a 1:1 meeting instead of inviting the whole team (I'll share more about who to invite later on in this chapter).

Even in these situations I strongly suggest that the audience has something to contribute. This might be a Q&A session to discuss the information, an instruction for everyone to consider the impact of the information on their work and a request to identify risks or issues to share with the managers after the meeting. In the discussion with your boss, include topics where their input, decisions, or advice are needed. When there is a chance for two way communication and some form of activity connected with the information the value of the meeting goes up.

So, before you hit "send" on that meeting invite, ask yourself: Do I really need to gather everyone in a room for this? If not, save everyone some time and find a better way.

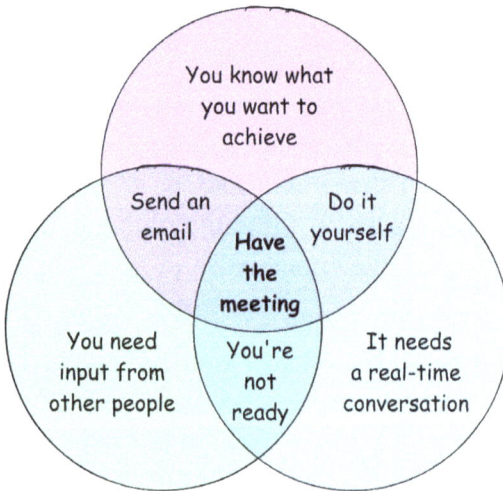

You know what you want to achieve

Send an email

Do it yourself

Have the meeting

You need input from other people

You're not ready

It needs a real-time conversation

CHAPTER 1

BEFORE THE MEETING

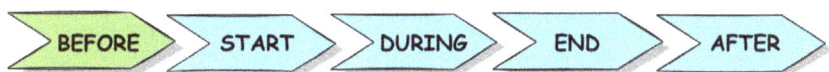

BEFORE ▸ START ▸ DURING ▸ END ▸ AFTER

You've probably heard the saying, "Failing to prepare is preparing to fail," and it couldn't be truer when it comes to meetings. To make sure your meeting isn't just another time suck, spend a few minutes doing these five things:

- » Get clear on the topic, purpose, and output.
- » Pick activities.
- » Include the right people.
- » Choose a location.
- » Write a great invitation.

To help you do these every time, download the Free Resource Kit found on the first page of this book, which includes a meeting planning template. Plus, at the end of this chapter you'll find some advice for situations where you are attending a meeting and not leading it.

> *Poor meeting culture is not the fault of executives, it's the fault of people who can't run meetings. Simple rule—no agenda or no clearly stated purpose? No meeting. Once everyone follows this rule you'd be surprised how efficient things get.*
> —Mash_man710

GET CLEAR ON THE TOPIC, PURPOSE, AND OUTPUT

If you can't clearly define what your meeting is about, why you're having it, and what you want to get out of it, stop right there—you're not ready to call a meeting.

Without a clear topic, purpose, and output, how will you invite the right participants? How will you know what to focus on? Or how will you tell if the meeting was successful? Spoiler: You won't. Research even backs this up—meetings with a clear purpose are way more effective.[1]

» **Topic:** What's the main thing you're going to talk about? Is it next month's sales targets? Kicking off a new project? Or maybe dealing with a tricky customer situation? Always make sure you know exactly what the focus is.

» **Purpose:** Why are you having this meeting? What do you want to achieve? Think of it like this: Your purpose is the "why" that gives your meeting direction. A strong purpose usually involves action, whether you're solving a problem, planning something, or making a decision.

» **Output:** This is what you're going to walk out of the meeting with. It's the tangible result, like a plan, a decision, or a list of actions. If you can't pin down what the output is, your meeting might end up just being a chat that goes nowhere.

---

1 https://doodle.com/en/resources/research-and-reports-/the-state-of-meetings-2019/

To get your next meeting right, answer these three questions:

1. What's the *topic*?
2. What is the *purpose* of this meeting?
3. What's the *output*?

That's it! You don't need to write much for each question. A few words or a sentence is usually enough. Here are some examples:

Practical Example 1

Let's say you're planning a meeting to choose which of two projects to start first. Here's how you could define it:

TOPIC:	PURPOSE:	OUTPUT:
Project priority choice	To decide which project will start first	The decision

Practical Example 2

You need to have a meeting to revise a budget as a result of recent cuts. By getting clear on these three things, you can invite the right people and pick the best activities to achieve the purpose and output.

TOPIC:	PURPOSE:	OUTPUT:
Next month's budget	To adjust the budget plan after recent cuts	A revised budget for next month

> *There was a meeting last week with no agenda and nothing in the invite, so we all showed up clueless. The organizer spent the first fifteen minutes figuring out what we should talk about. They forgot to tell us why we were there. The meeting ended, and I still didn't know what we were supposed to have done. They really should work this stuff out in advance.*
>
> —**Jenna, Product Manager**

WHAT ARE WE HERE TO DO?

While there can be a near infinite number of reasons, topics, and outputs for work meetings, most meetings fall into a small set of purpose categories:

- Information Gathering
- Idea Generation
- Decision-Making
- Planning
- Problem Solving
- Team Building
- Feedback & Evaluation
- Training & Development
- Networking
- Conflict Resolution
- Alignment/Synchronization
- Informing
- Status Updates & Progress Tracking

One meeting type that's not on this list is sales meetings. If you're planning a sales meeting, this probably isn't the right book. Yes, some techniques in this book will help, but you'd get a better result reading something by Zig Zigler.

If you're wondering why persuading people isn't in the list, that's because persuasion is a technique used to achieve some of these other purposes. It is not a purpose by itself. We persuade people to make decisions the way we want, or to resolve a conflict one way or another. Besides, you are not likely to get the result you want if your meeting invitation says "Purpose: To Persuade Jim to Do What I Want."

Remember the warning from chapter 1 about information-only meetings. There are very few situations where they add value. It is often better to use another form of communication to deliver the message.

HANDLING MULTIPLE TOPICS IN A MEETING

Multitopic meetings can get chaotic fast. Usually, the first topic eats up a lot of the available time, leaving the other topics to be rushed or ignored entirely. No one wants to sit through a meeting only to hear the leader say, "Sorry, we've run out of time for your topic. We'll have to push it to the next meeting." This is inefficient for people who are only there for the later topics, and no one wants to feel like their time was wasted.

This is why structure and prioritization are critical for successful multitopic meetings. Every subject should get the attention it deserves without dragging down the rest of the meeting.

To prioritize a multitopic meeting, start with the most important topic, the one with the biggest impact or urgency. It should also be the topic that involves the most people (see "Managing Partial Participants" in chapter 3 for more information). The remaining topics should be ordered using the same criteria: most impact, urgency, and number of people needed for the discussion

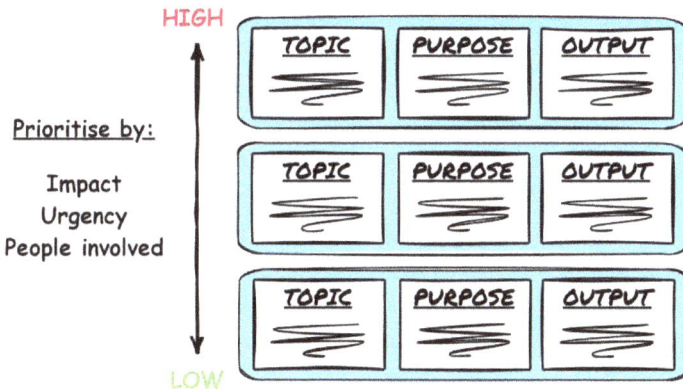

Be ready for the possibility that you might not get to every topic on your list. In fact, research shows the first topic almost always gets a disproportionate amount of time.[2]

---

2 Littlepage, G. E., and Poole, J. R., 1993, "Time Allocation in Decision Making Groups," *Journal of Social Behavior & Personality*, 8 (4), 663-72

PICKING THE RIGHT ACTIVITIES

Now that you've nailed down the purpose of your meeting and know what you want to get out of it, it's time to figure out how to make it happen. This is where picking the right activities comes in.

Think of activities as the engine that drives your meeting forward. They're the things you'll actually *do* during the meeting to get to your desired outcome. Whether it's coming up with ideas, holding votes to making decisions, or using a well-known model to help solve a problem, the right activities keep your meeting focused and productive.

Choosing the right activities is a game-changer. If you don't, your meeting might end up being all over the place, or worse—completely pointless. For example, if you're supposed to be making a decision but don't give people a chance to discuss the options, you're not likely to get an informed decision at the end.

HOW TO PICK THE RIGHT ACTIVITIES

Start with the basics. What's the purpose of your meeting, and what's the output you want? Once you've got that down, then choose activities that align with those goals. And remember, only include activities that directly help you achieve the meeting's purpose. If your goal is to choose between two options, choose activities that focus on reviewing and deciding.

There are *loads* of activities to choose from when planning your meeting. I've listed a *few* of them in the following table for the most common purposes. In most cases, activities from multiple categories will combine to produce the desired meeting output.

A quick online search will tell you what each activity is, or you can get a description of them, along with a much larger list of activities, for free on my website at www.chrisfenning.com/resources

Information Gathering: Surveys and Question-naires, Mind Mapping, Focus Groups, Data Reviews, and Brainstorming (*Uurgh—please try to avoid this!*)

Idea Generation: Starbursting, 5 Why's, Brainwriting (*this one is soooo much better than the storming version),* Six Thinking Hats, Fishbowl Discussion

Decision-Making: Presenting Information, Pros and Cons List, Dot Voting, Decision Matrix, Moscow Method

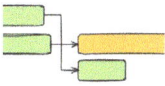

Planning: Milestone Mapping, Scenario Planning, Gantt Chart Creation, Back Casting, Timeline Creation

Problem Solving: Fishbone Diagram, Nominal Group Technique, Force Field Analysis, Consensus Workshop, Gap Analysis

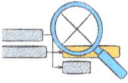

Status Updates & Progress Tracking: Traffic Light Reporting, Milestone Review, Kanban Board Review, One Sentence Updates, Successes and Challenges

Feedback & Evaluation: Start, Stop, Continue, Postmortem Discussion, Plus/Delta Discussion, Retrospective Circle, Surveys

Conflict Resolution: Conflict Mapping, Guided Discussion, Mediation, Interest-Based Negotiation, Collaborative Problem Solving,

I also highly recommend the book *Mission Critical Meetings: 81 Practical Facilitation Techniques* by Ava S. Butler. It's packed full of useful activities and tips for how to get the best results out of meetings.

Once you've chosen your activities, think about the tools and methods you'll use. For example, if you're voting, will you use a digital poll or a show of hands? The right method depends on whether your meeting is online, in person, or a combination of both. If you have a hybrid meeting with some people in a room and some online, make sure everyone can get involved. There's no point running a voting poll if four people in a room can only vote once on the group laptop.

Practical Example

Let's say you're setting up a meeting to review options and make a decision. Here's how you might structure the activities

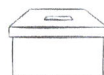

| 1. Clarify the objective | 2. Define Decision Criteria | 3. Present Options | 4. Discussion | 5. Vote and Decision |

1. **Clarify the Objective:** Make sure everyone knows what the decision is for.
2. **Define the Decision Criteria:** Agree on the criteria you'll use to make the decision.
3. **Present Options:** Start with a quick rundown of the options, either with a slideshow or a handout.
4. **Discussion**: Open up the floor for a discussion so everyone understands the pros and cons of each option.
5. **Vote and Decide:** Wrap it up with a vote to choose the best option.

By aligning your activities with the purpose and output, you'll keep your meeting on track and ensure it's actually worth everyone's time.

ACTIVITY

REVIEW YOUR ACTIVITIES

Past Meetings: Look at your work calendar, find a recent meeting you organized, and answer the following questions:

» Did you plan the activities needed to achieve the output?

» In hindsight, did all of the meeting activities support the output?

If you answered NO to either question, what would you do differently if you ran the meeting again?

Future Meetings: Look at an invitation you have sent for a meeting happening soon. If you haven't sent any invitations yet, think about a meeting you will have soon.

» Have you planned the activities for the meeting?

» Do all the activities support the creation of the output?

» List three different activities you can use to achieve the desired output.

» Which activity, or activities, best suits the purpose, location, and time available for the meeting?

When you have the right activities, you can mention them in the invitation. A little detail about the meeting format helps people prepare and shows that you are prepared too.

INCLUDE THE RIGHT PEOPLE

When you're organizing a meeting, who you invite matters a *lot*. Each person should either help you achieve the meeting's goal or get something valuable out of being there. If not, they probably don't need to be there.

Inviting the wrong people can cause the following side effects:

1. No desired output	2. Wasted time	3. More meetings	4. Damaged reputation	5. Wasted money

1. **No Desired Output:** Without the right people, you won't get the results you need.
2. **Wasted Time:** Inviting irrelevant participants can lead to off-topic chatter and wasted time.
3. **More Meetings:** If your meeting doesn't achieve its goal, you'll likely need a follow-up, which means more time and energy spent.
4. **Damaged Reputation:** Constantly running unproductive meetings can hurt how others view your planning skills.
5. **Wasted Money:** Every person in that meeting is being paid for their time. If the meeting isn't necessary, that's money down the drain.

Let's talk numbers. Imagine a 1-hour weekly meeting with 10 people, each making $30 an hour. That's $300 per meeting. Multiply that by 50 weeks and you're looking at $15,000 a year. Now, picture a bigger meeting with senior managers. It can easily cost $15,000 for a single two-hour session. And don't even get me started on company-wide meetings. They can cost tens of thousands of dollars just in employee time.

What surprises me is how companies tightly control spending on things like travel or office supplies, yet often let anyone schedule a meeting and invite whomever they want, no questions asked.

Here's an idea. If you want to highlight the cost of bad meetings in your company, include an estimate of the cost in the invitation. That should help everyone focus a little more on the value of their contribution. The point isn't to obsess over the exact cost of every meeting but to make sure the time spent is worth it. After all, people are getting paid whether they're in your meeting or not. The goal is to ensure their time in the meeting is more valuable than whatever they would be doing otherwise.

So next time you're planning a meeting, take a second to think about the cost in terms of people's time and whether it's really necessary to invite everyone on your list.

HOW TO PICK THE RIGHT PARTICIPANTS

When deciding who to invite, consider these three things:

1. **Knowledge of the Topic:** Does this person need to know about or already understand the topic?

2. **Ability to Achieve the Purpose:** Can this person help you reach the meeting's goal? This includes decision-makers, experts, and those who will carry out the work. Confirming each participant's ability to contribute to the purpose may require spending a little time contacting people before the meeting.

3. **Contribution to the Output:** Will this person help produce the outcome you need?

By picking the right people, you set your meeting up for success. And by avoiding unnecessary invites, you keep it focused, efficient, and productive. the goal is to keep your meetings lean. Research shows that for every person you add beyond seven, decision-making efficiency drops by 10 percent.[3] For creative meetings, more people can be useful, but keep in mind that larger groups mean less time for each person to contribute meaningfully. Once you hit twenty people, reading body language and managing the group gets tricky.[4]

Final Thought: One question I often hear is, "What about people who are interested and just want to listen to the meeting?" My response is simple and direct. Only invite people who will actively contribute to creating the desired output. What value does the business get from having passive observers sitting in on meetings they aren't contributing to? It's like seeing a group of people fixing a road—two people are digging a hole and the other five are standing around watching them. What an unproductive waste of time. This is one of the reasons so many people have full calendars and complain that they have too many meetings. Meeting participants should be contributors, not observers.

WHO SHOULD BE IN YOUR MEETING?

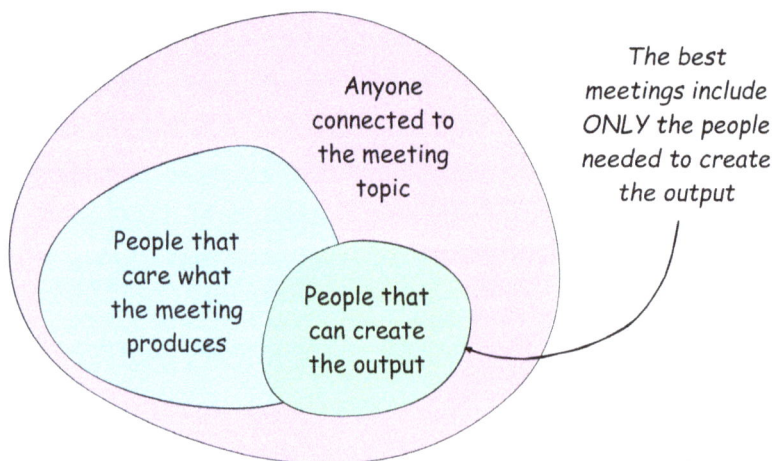

Anyone connected to the meeting topic

People that care what the meeting produces

People that can create the output

The best meetings include ONLY the people needed to create the output

3 https://www.bain.com/insights/decision-insights-9-decision-focused-meetings/
4 Paul Axtell, interviewed for Harvard Business Review, July 2015, https://hbr.org/2015/07/the-condensed-guide-to-running-meetings

ACTIVITY

REVIEW PARTICIPANTS

Look at three recent meetings you set up:

» Did every participant contribute to the output?

» Did you have everyone you needed?

» Was every participant needed for the entire meeting?

» If some people weren't needed for the entire meeting, did you thank them for attending in spite of this?

If your answer was NO for any question, what was the impact to the meeting efficiency and the desired output? What would you do differently if you planned the meeting again?

Next Step: Look at invitations you've sent for future meetings and do these things:

» Confirm all participants will contribute to the desired output.

» Remove participants who are not needed to create the output.

» If anyone is only contributing a small amount, consider contacting them before the meeting to thank them for taking part or arranging the meeting topics so they can leave after their part is complete. This can go a long way toward improving their engagement in the discussion. (Element 11 includes more options for handling partial participants.)

CONSIDER THE ACTIVITIES AND PEOPLE AGAIN

Having picked the activities and the people for your meeting, it's time to look at the two elements together. They both impact the success of your meeting and must complement each other. If there is a mismatch there will be consequences.

Consider a situation where you bring your team together to find a solution to a problem. The activities in the meeting may include idea generation, discussion, debate, voting, and some way to make a decision. All the activities help your team create ideas and select a good option. In addition to the team members, you invite your manager because your meeting purpose is to leave with an approved decision.

The activities are the right ones for the purpose of the meeting, but they don't match all of the people invited to it. Is your manager needed for the entire process? If they only need to approve the final decision, is it the best use of their time? Probably not. Plus, their presence may influence the activities. Team members may be less willing to speak up with unconventional or riskier ideas out of worry about looking stupid in front of the boss. In this situation it would be better to remove the manager from the idea-generation meeting. Have either a one-on-one conversation with them later, or schedule another, much shorter meeting to present the proposal and get approval.

A quick sanity check of the activities and people can highlight issues like the one described above. Consider their level, experience, and what they will contribute. Always check if the activities match the expected contribution of each participant.

> *We had a meeting scheduled to discuss updates on our project. Something like fifteen people were invited, and it turned into a chaotic mess. Half the people weren't supposed to be involved with the project, and they kept side-tracking the discussion with unrelated questions. If they'd picked the right participants, it could have been a quick conversation instead of a waste of almost two hours.*
> —**Marcus, Project Coordinator**

HOW LONG SHOULD A MEETING BE?

Meetings can last a few minutes or many hours, but most are 30 to 60 minutes long. Why? Because that's the default length of time most calendar tools use for meeting duration.

When planning your meeting, don't use a default length unless you have thought about it first. Think about what you need to achieve and the activities needed to produce the output. Then choose the smallest amount of time necessary to produce the output while still being realistic. Conversations almost always take longer than we expect.

To select the right meeting length, sketch out a rough timeline that includes the introduction, activities, and a wrap-up. *(You can find more on the specific steps for a wrap-up in later chapters.)*

Example Plan:

Meeting section	Duration (mins)
Introduction	5
Activity 1	10
Activity 2	5
Activity 3	15
Wrap-up	5

For this meeting the duration should be 45 minutes. This including time for all the activities plus a few spare minutes not assigned to specific activities.

Every time we set up a meeting, we are guessing how much time it will take. Leave some wiggle room rather than fill every minute of your agenda with activities. If you don't allow enough time, you'll try to control the clock too much. You're more likely to cut off important conversations and frustrate everyone involved. Allow time for discussions, unexpected questions, and yes, even allow time for those long-winded folks who always seem to have something to say. (Check out chapter 4 for ways to keep those long-winded folks on track). Plus, as a bonus, allowing a little extra time for each activity means you might even finish early.

For multitopic meetings, decide how much time each topic needs and make sure it fits within the meeting duration you schedule. If you don't have enough time, you might need to cut a topic or adjust your approach. If different people are leading different topics, check with them beforehand to make sure their sections will fit within the time you'll allocate. Remember to also ask what activities they plan to use to produce the output. This will give you a good idea whether they can be achieved in the available time. If not, have a conversation to talk about alternative activities or how to adjust the meeting topic list to ensure the meeting doesn't overrun.

Example Multitopic Plan

Meeting section	Time
Introduction	5
Topic 1 – Project Update (Sarah) Activity = Presentation of changes	10
Topic 2 – Risk Review (Rajesh) Activity 1 = Update risk log & prioritize Activity 2 = Review and update top 5 risks	10
Topic 3 – Budget Review (Jan) Activity 1 = Identify budget impacts from project changes Activity 2 =Present changes and identify any increases Activity 3 = Summarize impact and decide if we need to request more budget	20
Wrap-up	5
Buffer / Spare Time	10
Total Meeting Duration	60

CHOOSING A LOCATION

When it comes to picking a location for your meeting, the choice is usually pretty straightforward. If everyone's in the same office, you'll probably book a meeting room. But if your team is scattered across different cities—or even countries—a virtual meeting is the way to go. Do you have a mix of both? Then a hybrid meeting is probably the way to go.

The activities you choose will influence your choice of venue. You need to consider the location while picking the activities. There's no point choosing a physical activity if everyone is online, and vice versa. For example, if you want to use physical objects like flip charts and stickers for dot voting, you need people to be together in the same room.

"But what about workshops and team retreats?"

If you have this question, check out the recommended reading section at the end of the book. This guide is all about the everyday meetings you handle as part of your job. The ones that fill your calendar day in and day out.

WRITE A GREAT INVITATION

If you've followed the steps so far, you should have all the ingredients for a great invitation. Invitations play a big part in the success of a meeting, but they're often overlooked. Think about the last time you got a vague or blank meeting invite. Did you feel ready and informed? Probably not. A well-crafted invitation sets the tone for your meeting. Without it, you're inviting poor attendance, confusion, frustration, and wasted time.

Here's what happens when you send out a blank or vague invite:

Poor Attendance: If your invite is unclear, people might skip it or choose another meeting over yours.

Confusion: Vague invites leave everyone guessing about what's going on.

Frustration: Nobody likes feeling unprepared or unsure of why they're even attending.

Wasted Time: Meetings without clear invites tend to go off the rails, wasting time and leading to more meetings to fix what went wrong.

In short, bad invitations lead to bad meetings. The worst kind of bad invitation is the one that says almost nothing at all. The dreaded blank invite....Please, please, I beg of you, *please*, don't send blank meeting invitations.

Imagine a coworker walks up to you and says, "Be in meeting room 2 at 10:30 tomorrow," then just walks away. No explanation, no context. It's more like a summons than an invitation. You'd probably feel annoyed, perhaps even a bit anxious. I doubt you're looking forward to a productive conversation, and the curiosity inspired by this invite will likely be distracting until the purpose of the meeting is known.

If you want your meeting to start off on the right foot, your invite needs to be more than just a date, time, and subject line. Nobody wants to feel like they're being summoned to a meeting or left wondering about what lies ahead in their workday.

HOW TO WRITE A GREAT INVITATION

The good news is that writing a solid invitation is easy. Here's what to include:

1. **Subject Line:** Clearly state the meeting topic and purpose.
   - o Example: "Project Everest: Identifying Team Members"
   - o Example: "Staff Outing: Confirming the Date"

2. **Body of the Invitation:** Cover the topic, purpose, output, and any prep work attendees need to do.
   - o **Topic**: What's the meeting about?
   - o **Purpose**: Why are you having this meeting?
   - o **Output**: What will the meeting produce?
   - o **Preparation**: What do attendees need to do or bring?

These details make sure everyone knows what they are being invited to, what's expected, and how to prepare.

> *I received a meeting invite for 'Important Team Discussion.' I moved a client meeting to attend, only to find it was about a minor branding change. Half of us didn't need to be there. I could have been doing real work and helping my client. Why can't people write better invitations?*
> —**Alicia, Marketing Analyst**

Practical Example

Say you're setting up a meeting for a new project, Project Everest. You need to identify team members for key roles. The example over the page shows how your invite might look:

TO	
TITLE	Project Everest: Creating the project team
DATE		TIME	
LOCATION	

TOPIC = Creating the Project Everest team.

PURPOSE = Identify people to work on the new project.

OUTPUT = A list of names for key project roles.

HOW TO PREPARE = Come prepared with your team's availability for the next three months.

This invite tells people exactly what to expect and how to prepare, which means your meeting will be more focused and effective.

NOTE: If you need or expect people to prepare something for a meeting, I have some shocking news for you—some people don't read meeting invitations. Don't assume everyone will prepare just because the invitation says so. Contact people directly by phone, message, email, or in person and make sure they are aware of the need to prepare. This may seem like extra work up front, but it will avoid a lot more work later when people turn up unprepared.

Keep it Short and Sweet

Meeting invitations don't need to be long—shorter is often better. A concise invite is more likely to be read and understood.

Create a Template

If your calendar app allows it, create a template for new meetings. Include prompts for the topic, purpose, output, and preparation so you'll have a reminder to include all the important details every time you set up a meeting.

By following these simple steps, you'll send out invitations that get people prepared, focused, and ready to contribute, setting the stage for a successful meeting.

VALIDATE PARTICIPANTS AND UNDERSTANDING

Careful planning is great, but things change. People move to new jobs or there may be a better expert to invite to the conversation.

Imagine starting your meeting only to find you need someone else to provide detail on a topic. Or the participants didn't agree with or understand the topic you want to discuss. That's a surefire way to reduce meeting effectiveness.

To avoid any unpleasant surprises, it's worth checking with the participants before the meeting. Make sure they understand the meeting topic and purpose and check that they don't have any questions and agree the right people are involved. This isn't needed for every invitation you send, but the more important the meeting, the more valuable this step is. A quick message, email, or call to the critical people in the invitation is all it takes. You'll quickly identify if there is anything you should do before the meeting to ensure its success.

WHEN YOU DON'T HAVE ALL THE DETAILS

Sometimes you need to set up a meeting before you've got everything figured out, maybe just to block out time on everyone's calendar. In these cases, keep the invitation clear but general. For example:

> » "This is a placeholder for a meeting about [topic] and [purpose]. Full details to come before the meeting."

Just make sure you remember to send those details later!

WHEN YOU'RE NOT LEADING THE MEETING

What if you're on the receiving end of a meeting invitation and it's... well, pretty useless? Maybe it's blank or doesn't tell you anything about what the meeting's for. It's a red flag that you might be in for a timewaster.

But don't worry—you've got a couple of options to turn things around before you waste an hour of your time.

» **Option 1: Ask for More Info.** If the invitation doesn't include the topic, purpose, or expected output, don't sit there wondering. Reach out to the organizer and ask for the missing details. You deserve to know what you're walking into so you can a) prepare and b) decide if it's worth your time. After all, it's called an invitation, not a summons. Even better, suggest that the organizer update the invitation for everyone. Chances are, you're not the only one in the dark.

» **Option 2: Decline the Invitation.** If you don't feel like playing detective, you can simply decline the meeting. But here's the key—always add a note explaining why. A blank decline is just as annoying as a blank invite.

When I led a project management team, we were bombarded with multiple invites for the same time slots. Without clear information, we couldn't figure out which meetings to attend, so we made it a rule to automatically decline blank invites.

At first, people were hesitant, especially when the invites came from higher-ups in the company. To smooth the transition, we spent two weeks setting expectations. Anytime someone got a vague or blank invite, they'd ask the sender for more details and say that future blank invites would be declined. I also let the other managers know about our new rule. The result? Within two weeks, almost every invitation included information on the meeting's topic and purpose.

Not only was it easier to choose which meetings to attend but the meetings themselves were better. People came prepared, and meetings were more likely to produce what they needed.

So, if you get invited to a meeting and the invite is a mess, don't be shy. Ask for more info, or if you're feeling gutsy, hit decline. It might be the push the organizer needs to step up their game.

PLAN FOR THE MINUTES AND NOTES

Meeting minutes and notes are created during the meeting and that means you need to prepare before the meeting. It doesn't take much effort to prepare, but it's important you can answer these questions:

» **Who will take the meeting minutes?** Will you do it or will you ask someone else to take them?

» **How detailed do they need to be?** Do you need a full transcript or just a list of actions and decisions? (By the way, unless you're taking notes for a legal deposition, you aren't going to need a complete transcript of the discussion. No one outside the room cares what Derek from Marketing said in response to Cara from Finance about next Thursday's client lunch.)

» **Will you use automation and AI tools?** Many applications like Otter.ai, Fathom, and Zoom include automated AI-based note taking features. These can work even for in-person meetings as long as someone has a laptop or phone running the app. They also provide recordings of the entire conversation just in case someone wants to relive the excitement of a discussion.

For more information about creating and sharing short, useful notes, check out Chapter 5.

ACTIVITY

HOW CLEAR ARE YOUR INVITATIONS?

Look at your work calendar and find five recent meetings you organized and sent the invitation for.

- Do the invitations have information in the main body?
- Did they all include a clear topic?
- Did they all state the meeting purpose?
- Did they include the desired outcome or output?

If you answered YES for each question, well done. You have already been creating good meeting invitations. If you answered NO for any of the questions, don't worry, you now know the areas to focus on improving.

Thinking about the questions where you answered NO, what will you do differently in your next invitation to make it clearer?

NOTE: This activity is better when using your own examples, but if you don't have any meetings of your own, you can use invitations sent by other people. If you are using invitations written by other people, you can still answer the questions but do so as an assessor of the other person's invitation content.

CHAPTER 2

STARTING THE MEETING

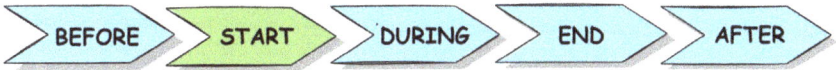

| BEFORE | START | DURING | END | AFTER |

Starting a meeting well takes less than two minutes and has only two steps. But, these steps are so important that they get their own chapter. What are they?

1. Introduce the meeting.
2. Validate with the participants.

Get these steps right and your chances of a successful meeting go way up. Get them wrong and, yes, you guessed it, the meeting is probably going to fail.

Luckily these steps are both easy and quick. One to two minutes is all you need.

INTRODUCE THE MEETING

When people walk into your meeting, they might still be thinking about their last task, another meeting, or their weekend plans. Your job is to refocus their attention on the meeting at hand.

The clearest way to do this is to start by introducing the topic, purpose, and output (TPO) and saying how much time the meeting will take. It's simple, effective, and helps everyone get on the same page from the start.

By kicking things off with TPO, you help everyone understand why they're there, what they need to do, and what the meeting should accomplish. Adding the comment about time shows the attendees you're paying attention to the clock and planning not to overrun.

If you skip the TPO introduction, you risk having participants who, instead of being productively focused, might be wondering:

» Why are we here?

» What are we supposed to do?

» What are we expected to produce?

» How long will this take?

When people don't know the answers to these questions, they quickly become confused and lose focus. That leads to frustration, off-topic discussions, and possibly the need for more meetings later on—all things you want to avoid.

> *There was a meeting last week with no agenda and nothing useful in the invite. Half the people there seemed to know what it was about because right away they started talking about some big issue a client had raised. The meeting ended, and I still didn't know what we were supposed to have done. They really should define the purpose in advance.*
> —**Jenna, Product Manager**

The Importance Of A Great Introduction

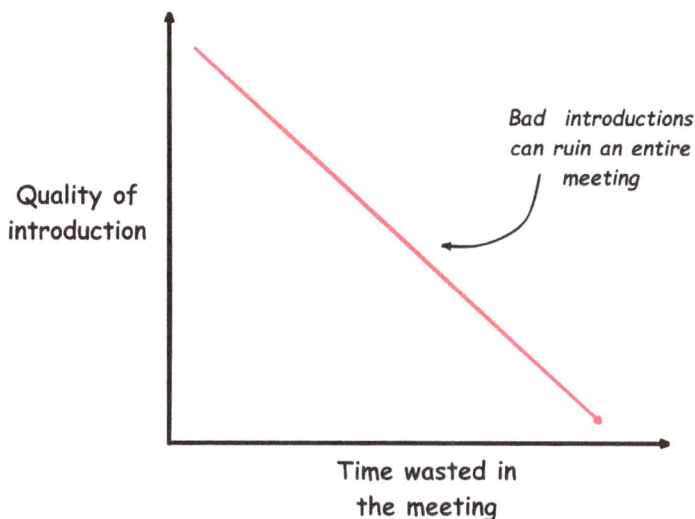

Quality of introduction

Bad introductions can ruin an entire meeting

Time wasted in the meeting

HOW TO INTRODUCE YOUR MEETING USING TOPIC, PURPOSE, OUTPUT

If you sent an invite that includes TPO, you have everything you need to introduce the meeting. For many years I have used the invitation as the meeting introduction. Not only does it contain the information everyone needs to get started but it also helps me focus on what we are about to do.

When jumping from meeting to meeting, it's easy to get things mixed up. A good TPO invitation tells me what I'm about to jump into, helps me quickly shift gears to the next thing I need to do in my work-day.

Try it with your own invitations using a script like this:

» **Greet the Participants:** "Hi, everyone, welcome to today's meeting."

- » **State the Topic:** "Today, we're going to talk about [topic]."

- » **Explain the Purpose:** "The reason we're here is to [purpose]."

- » **Define the Output:** "By the end of today's session, we will have [output]."

- » **Show the Relevance (optional):** "This matters because [explain why it's important to them]."

The last step isn't written in the invitation you sent. Usually, the TPO is enough to show why a meeting is relevant to the participants, but when it's not enough, you need to explain why it matters to them.

Include one or two sentences showing how the meeting's purpose and output will impact their work or goals. When participants see how a meeting is relevant to them, they're much more likely to be engaged and contribute.

Practical Example

Let's say you're leading a meeting to discuss results from a staff engagement survey. Here's how you might kick it off:

- » **Greeting:** "Hi, everyone, welcome to today's staff engagement feedback meeting."

- » **Topic:** "Today, we're going to talk about the results of the recent staff engagement survey."

- » **Purpose:** "We're here to share the survey results, discuss the company's response, and brainstorm ways our team can support the follow-up work."

- » **Output:** "By the end of today's session, we'll have identified the top five areas that need improvement, the top three areas that are already strong, and a list of ideas for how our team can help improve things over the next year."

- » **Relevance:** "This matters because improving these areas will not only make our workplace better but also be part of our goals for the upcoming year."

With this quick overview, everyone knows what to expect, what they need to do, and why it's important.

Is The Introduction Good Enough?

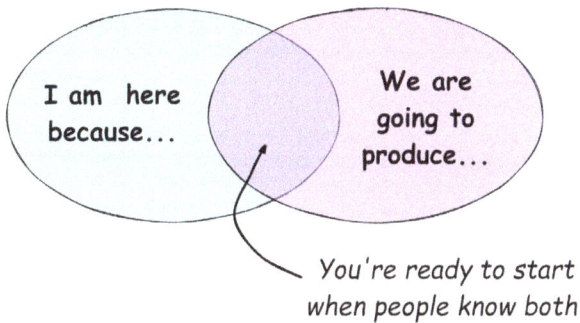

I am here because...

We are going to produce...

You're ready to start when people know both

FOR MULTITOPIC MEETINGS

If you have multiple topics in the meeting, start by stating how many topics you have and then give a very short summary of each topic's purpose and desired outcomes. Then begin each topic with a more detailed TPO as described above.

Example: "We have three things to cover today. We'll make sure everyone is up to date on the project changes, identify any new risks, and adjust the budget accordingly. Our first topic is the project update. The purpose is to ensure we all know what's changed and why and to answer any questions. I'll give a quick rundown of the changes, then we'll have about fifteen minutes for questions."

INTRODUCING PARTICIPANTS

There will be times when the meeting participants don't know each other. If this happens, do a quick summary of the people in the room.

I suggest avoiding the typical activity of going around the table, asking everyone to speak. That can take a long time and quite often people aren't sure what or how much to say. Instead, quickly name each participant, their team, and/or role, and one line about why they are included in the meeting. This not only speeds up the process but also reminds everyone why they are in the meeting and how they can contribute.

Example:

"We have a few new people joining us today. John is from Marketing and will help us avoid clashes between our promotion and the others planned across the company. Emma is from the IT team, supporting our new product. She is going to keep us realistic and make sure we don't create a marketing plan that makes the tech timeline impossible. Sajay, Freya, and Eva are all in the product development team and are the ones coming up with the promotion plan for the project."

MANAGING PARTIAL PARTICIPANTS

When your meeting covers multiple topics, some people might only need to be there part of the time. These are the people most likely to be annoyed if your meeting isn't efficient. Here are three ways to avoid frustrating them:

1. **Let People Leave When They're Done:** If the meeting is long and has distinct sections, arrange the topics so people can leave after their part is done. Mention this in the introduction to prepare everyone. *Example*: *"[Introduction]...Some of you only need to be here for the first two topics. When we're done with those, we'll pause and let you go. Sanjay and Claire, I'll let you know when that is. Anyone else?"*

2. **Acknowledge and Minimize Impact:** If people can't leave, acknowledge it and try to keep irrelevant topics short. *Example*: *"I know not all topics affect everyone, so thanks for your patience. We'll keep things moving quickly."*

3. **Follow the Inverse Time Rule:** When only a few people are involved in a topic, you are essentially having a meeting within a meeting. A good rule to follow is that the fewer people involved in a topic, the less time you should spend on it. If a lot of your meeting is irrelevant to many participants, seriously consider splitting it into separate meetings.

The Inverse Time Rule

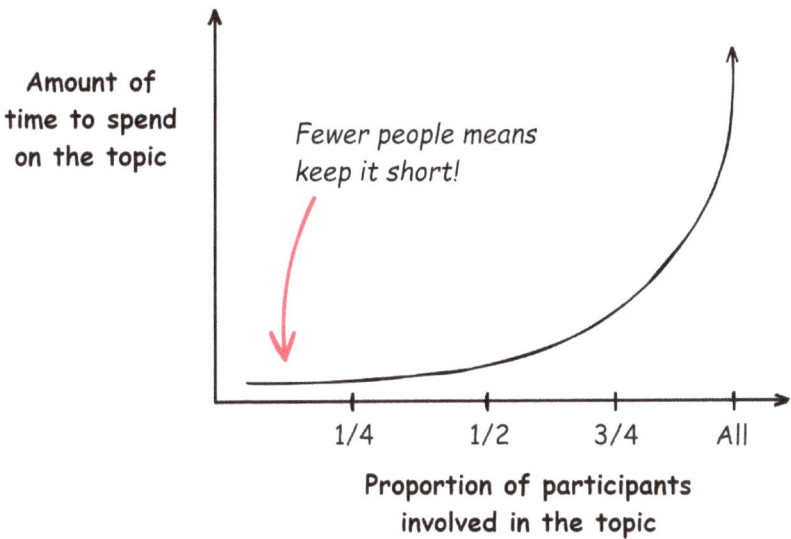

Amount of time to spend on the topic

Fewer people means keep it short!

1/4   1/2   3/4   All

Proportion of participants involved in the topic

This is more important if everyone is physically in a meeting room. If the meeting is online, the partial participants can just leave the call when their part is done and get on with other work.

When partial participants aren't given the option to leave, they can raise the topic. This is worth doing if there is at least half an hour left in the meeting. Ask the meeting leader, "Is there anything else for us to cover that I should be around for?" If the answer is NO, ask if it's okay to leave. Remember to leave quietly and minimize the disruption to the meeting.

WHAT IF YOU'RE NOT LEADING THE MEETING?

If you're a participant in a meeting and a few minutes in you still don't know what it's about, speak up! It doesn't matter what your role is or who's leading the meeting—if you're confused, others probably are too.

You could say something like, "Sorry if I missed this, but can we clarify the specific purpose of the meeting and what we're aiming to achieve by the end?" You might even add a prompt like, "Are we here to brainstorm solutions, or are we making a decision today?"

Clarity benefits everyone, so don't be afraid to ask for it.

WHAT IF SOMEONE ARRIVES LATE AND DISRUPTS THE MEETING?

Lateness happens, but it doesn't have to derail the entire meeting. Always aim to start on time. This sets a precedent for future meetings. If people enter the meeting late, don't make a big deal out of it. Continue the meeting without drawing attention to the latecomer. Then, at a natural pause in the flow, quickly recap what's been done to help the late arrival catch up. I'm not suggesting tardiness shouldn't be addressed, only that your group meeting isn't the time or place.

WHAT IF KEY DECISION-MAKERS ARE MISSING?

If someone crucial isn't there when you need to start, the first step is to find out if they will be joining. Contact the missing person to check if they're coming. Whatever the answer, you must decide how to proceed.

If they will only be a few minutes late, it's usually best to wait for them. If they will be significantly late, decide if you can make a start without them or if you must postpone the meeting. If the missing person isn't able to join at all, decide whether to postpone or if it's worth continuing with the people who are present to complete as much as possible without the decision-maker. In this case, part of your meeting should include making a plan for how to finalize the decisions later on.

VALIDATE WITH THE PARTICIPANTS

You are almost ready to get into the main part of the meeting. But before you do, there is one more thing to do. You must validate that you have the right people and they agree with the purpose and output.

You may have already done some validation after sending the invitation, as described earlier. But even if you did that step, a quick validation at the start of your meeting can save you from a lot of headaches. It's your chance to check two things:

1. That everyone is clear on why they are there and what they need to do.
2. You've got the right people in the room to achieve the meeting's purpose.

Skipping this step can lead to all sorts of problems, like distractions, disruptions, wrong outputs, frustrated participants, and even a hit to your reputation if the meeting goes off the rails.

This step is not just to give you confidence. It also gives your participants a chance to buy into the meeting's purpose, making them more likely to stay engaged and help achieve the desired outcome.

HOW TO VALIDATE WITH THE PARTICIPANTS

Validating with your participants is easy. Here's how you do it as part of the introduction:

» **Introduce the Meeting:** "Hi, everyone, today we're here to discuss [topic]. Our purpose is to [purpose], and by the end, we aim to produce [output]."

» **Ask for Confirmation:** "Can I check that nothing has changed and we still need to work on this [topic/purpose/output]?"

» **Check the People:** "Can I also do a final check that we have the right people to produce the output? If you feel you're not the right person to help with this, now's a great time to speak up so you can leave."

Checking that the right people are present is something you did (or should have done!) before the meeting, but things can change, invitations are forwarded, and people sometimes bring a friend with them. Offering people the chance to leave might seem risky, but it ensures only the essential folks stick around. Plus, who wouldn't appreciate being able to skip a meeting that's not relevant to them?

If you're worried about key people leaving because they don't see the relevance, be clear about why you invited them. For example, "If you feel this meeting isn't relevant to you, feel free to leave. Raj and Sophia, the reason I'd like you to stay is because you'll hear information that will impact your tasks later this month."

And if someone unexpected shows up—perhaps they got the invite forwarded to them—don't hesitate to ask why they're there. "Hi, Ahmed, I wasn't expecting to see you here today. While it's great to have you, I don't want to waste your time. Can you let me know what you're hoping to contribute or get from this?"

Let's say you've set up a meeting, and the invitation has been forwarded to several additional people. To avoid wasting anyone's time, you might start with something like:

"Hey, everyone, before we get started, I noticed this invitation was forwarded a few times and we have some extra attendees. Can I check we have the right people to be productive today? If it turns out this meeting isn't relevant to you, feel free to leave. Our topic today is [specific topic], the purpose is [specific purpose], and our desired output is [specific output]. Is this something you all need to be here for?"

By doing this, you give people the option to excuse themselves if they're not needed, keeping your meeting focused and efficient. In short, a quick validation step at the start of your meeting can make all the difference in keeping things on track and making sure everyone's time is well spent.

When the meeting includes more than one topic, you can also ask if the topics are still in the right order. Example: "Before we dive in, does this list still make sense? Are these topics in the best order?"

BUT WHAT ABOUT AGENDAS?

Wait a minute, you might be thinking, *don't meetings need agendas?*

Ah, the agenda—the magical solution that makes every meeting perfect. Sure, there's some evidence that agendas can help,[1] but here's the thing—an agenda on its own won't save a meeting. Most agendas are just a list of topics, speakers, and time slots, which doesn't set you up for success.

The problem with standard agendas is that they often lack the most important details—the purpose of the meeting and what you're supposed to get out of it. When you've just got a list of topics and names, it's easy for speakers to ramble without a clear focus and attendees aren't given much to prepare with. Ideally, every speaker would kick off their section with the purpose and desired outcome, but let's be honest, that doesn't always happen.

Another issue with typical agendas is that they rely too much on the meeting organizer. If the organizer can't make it, whoever steps in is left with a vague script that doesn't offer much guidance. You end up with a meeting leader saying something like, "Uh, Jane, it's your turn to talk about the budget," which doesn't exactly scream "productive meeting."

---

1 Leach et al., 2009, "Perceived Meeting Effectiveness: The Role of Design Characteristics," *Journal of Business Psychology*, 24 (1), 65-76

So, what's the alternative? Use the meeting invitation! You've already included the topic, purpose, and output (TPO) in there, so why complicate things with a separate document? If you've got multiple topics or your company insists on using a formal agenda, go ahead and make one, but make sure it's a TPO format agenda. List each topic with its purpose and output and maybe add the name of the person leading that segment of the meeting if it's not you. That way, anyone can run the meeting effectively even if they're stepping in at the last minute.

Here's a pro tip Caterina Kostoula describes in her book, *Hold Successful Meetings*.[2] Instead of just listing topics, frame them as questions. For example, would you rather attend a meeting with "Budget Review" on the agenda, or one with "How can we increase our profitability by 10 percent?" The second one is way more engaging because it gets people thinking right away.

I'm not totally against agendas, but I am against pointless lists that don't actually help the meeting. If you're going to create an agenda, make sure it's something that will truly guide the discussion.

If the idea of a meeting without a traditional agenda feels wrong, there is a middle ground. After defining the topic, purpose, and output, provide the meeting participants with a draft agenda. Then ask them to add the questions and subtopics they feel should be included in the meeting. This collaborative agenda approach has a number of benefits.

» First, it makes everyone partially responsible for the meeting running smoothly because they approved and contributed to the topics being discussed.

» Second, it gives you a tool to fight tangential, less relevant side-topics during the meeting. As soon as the conversation goes off track, you can point out the topic isn't on the "collaborative agenda" and bring the meeting back on track. If someone wants to discuss a specific topic, they should have put it in the agenda beforehand.

---

2 Caterina Kostoula, 2021, *Hold Successful Meetings*, Penguin Business Experts

BUT WHAT ABOUT STARTING ON TIME?

What if people show up late, or don't show up at all? If your meeting is well-planned, you'll need everyone there to get started, especially since the introduction is crucial for setting the tone and direction. Starting on time isn't always within your control though.

Of course, it's great to start on time, and you should definitely aim to do so as soon as everyone's present. But if you find yourself waiting a few minutes, use that time wisely. Chat with the people who are there and strengthen those connections. Whether it's a casual conversation or a quick team-building activity, make the most of the wait time.

For some great ideas on quick activities, check out Christopher Littlefield's book, *75+ Team Building Activities for Remote Teams*. It's packed with simple, effective ways to build trust and improve communication whether you're meeting in person or online.

So, yes, agendas and punctuality matter, but they're not the be-all and end-all. Focus on what really makes meetings work: clarity, purpose, and making the best use of everyone's time.

ASSESSMENT:

HOW DO YOU INTRODUCE MEETINGS?

Here's a quick way to check if your meeting introductions are top notch or if there is room for improvement. Think about the last meeting you led and answer the following questions:

» Did you have the introduction prepared before the meeting?

» Did you tell the participants why they were all included?

» Did the introduction include a clear description of the output?

» Did the participants all agree they were needed for the meeting?

» Did everyone agree with the meeting purpose and output?

For any questions you answered NO to, what was the impact on the meeting? What will you do differently in your next meeting to avoid that impact?

CHAPTER 3

DURING THE MEETING

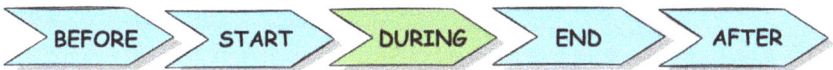

BEFORE START DURING END AFTER

Once your meeting is underway, maintaining focus, managing time, and ensuring progress toward your goals are essential to achieving a successful outcome. This section provides you with the tools and techniques needed to navigate the dynamic nature of meetings and keep them on track.

> *Once, we were dragged into an hour-long meeting about system upgrades. The meeting went off topic almost immediately, as people talked about everything from minor user issues to complaints about a totally different system not even related to the upgrade. Nobody kept us on track, and we left without covering the upgrade plan. Just another typical meeting.*
> —**Sam, Software Developer**

THE COST OF LOSING FOCUS

Every conversation in the meeting should contribute to achieving the purpose and producing the output. When discussions drift off course, time gets wasted and everyone leaves frustrated. Losing focus means you are likely to experience one or more of these problems:

Running Out of Time: You might realize too late that the meeting is almost over, forcing a rushed ending.

Incomplete Output: Spending too much time on one part of the discussion can mean you don't cover everything needed to achieve the goal(s).

Needing Another Meeting: If you don't finish in time, you'll have to schedule another meeting, which is frustrating for everyone.

Whether you have fifteen minutes or three hours, you need to monitor both your time and how close you are to achieving your meeting's goal. Regularly checking the time and progress helps you stay on track and make necessary adjustments.

HOW TO STAY ON TIME

You know you need to keep things on track, but saying it is one thing and doing it quite another. Keeping a conversation moving at the right pace can be tricky, especially when conversations naturally twist and turn. The simplest way to keep things on track is to think of your meeting as a journey and follow these steps:

» **Set the Target and Duration:** At the start, clearly state the output you want and the time you have available. For example,

"We have one hour to come up with five options for our project." Remember, the actual time for discussion is less than the total meeting time because of the introduction and wrapping up.

» **Observe the Journey:** Let the conversation flow but keep an eye on whether it's moving toward your goal. Guide without forcing things. As long as progress is being made toward the output, some flexibility is okay.

» **Check Time Against Progress:** Keep an eye on how much time has passed. Does it match the plan you created before the meeting? Are you on track to achieve the output? For example, if you're halfway through the meeting time, are you halfway to achieving your goal?

» **Adjust if Needed:** If the conversation is not moving fast enough, you need to speed things up or cut off side discussions. For instance, "We've discussed one option so far, and we're halfway through the meeting. We need to pick up the pace to cover the remaining options and make a decision."

» **Give Time Updates:** When everyone knows how much time is

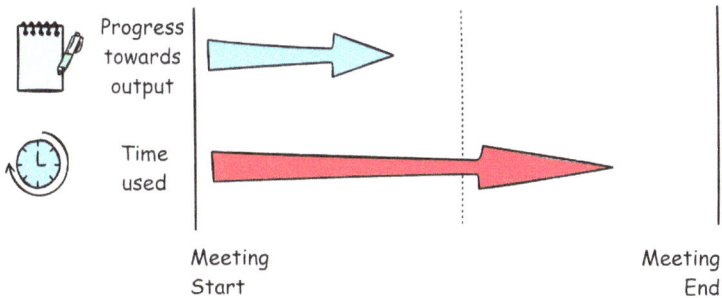

| Progress towards output | Meeting Start |
| Time used | Meeting End |

left, it's easier for the group to stay on track and focused. This makes the leader's job easier.

» **Continue to the Output:** Keep monitoring the discussion and be ready to adjust again if needed.

If there are multiple topics, repeat the process for each.

Practical Example

Your meeting aims to finalize five action items that you made clear at the start. Midway through the available time, you realize the discussion has only addressed one item. Here's how you could adjust the meeting from the moment you realize something needs to change.

» **Remind People About the Target Output:** "We started this meeting with the goal of finalizing five action items today."

» **Highlight the Issue:** "We've spent a lot of time on the first item. Looking at what is left to cover, I don't think we have enough time to cover all four of the remaining actions."

» **Decide On the Adjustment:** "We can either continue as planned or prioritize the most critical items. My preference is to prioritize and ensure we get the most important items finished today. Do you agree?"

» **Communicate Adjustments:** "Okay, so we all agree, we'll prioritize the top two items to ensure we complete the most important tasks."

» **Have a Plan for the Original TPO:** "If there's time after that, we can do the last two, and if we don't get to them, I will set up another meeting with only the people working on them."

HOW TO SPEED THINGS UP

There are many reasons conversations slow down. Here are some common ones with suggestions for how to speed things up again.

Everyone Has a Story to Share:

Time can disappear when people want to share their experience on a topic or issue. While it's important to allow space for this type of discussion, there is little value in hearing three or more examples of the same thing. If you're meeting becomes an "I have a story about that..." session, here are some phrases you could try:

» "I am hearing lots of great examples and see a few of you are eager to share. For the sake of time, can we move the conversation into how we can solve the problem?"

» "It seems like we could talk about this issue all day—it's clearly a problem. Let's summarize what's been said so far and move onto planning how to fix it."

Someone Repeats the Same Issue:

When someone keeps bringing up the same point and slowing down the progress, try one or more of these:

» **Acknowledge and Move On:** "Thanks for the reminder. We addressed that earlier by [resolution]."

» **Ask a Question**: "Is there something more about this issue that we're missing?"

» **Create Time for Later:** "Let's talk more about this after we've covered our main agenda items."

The Conversation Gets Too Detailed or Technical:

When discussions start to get deep into specifics, they can slip away. Before doing anything, always assess the need for the detail. Is the detailed talk necessary? If yes, keep it brief and thank others for their patience. If not, try one of these approaches to speed things up.

» **Suggest a Separate Meeting:** "This seems to be a deep dive. Can we schedule time for that separately?"

» **Summarize and Move On:** Give a quick overview of the key points and move back to the main agenda.

» **Follow-Up Documents:** Suggest detailed follow-ups in writing for those interested.

If you choose to go with separate meetings or follow up documents, they become actions from the meeting. Make sure they are noted and someone is assigned to set up the meeting by a specific date and time.

The Group Can't Seem to Move On:

Sometimes a conversation gets stuck with lots of enthusiastic contributions from the group. Give things a nudge with these phrases:

- » "I think we're spending more time on this than planned. Can we move to the next item?"
- » "Do we have enough information to make a decision on this now?"
- » "Can we do a quick vote or consensus check and move on?"
- » "That's a good point, but it might be better addressed after we've completed [desired output]."
- » "Let's speed this up so we don't have to schedule another meeting."

HOW TO KEEP THE CONVERSATION ON TRACK

Speed is not the only thing that causes problems. Meetings are more likely to fail when the conversation goes off track. Unless you run your meetings with an iron fist (please don't!), conversations are rarely a straight line from start to end. There are twists and turns as different people contribute to the discussion. Activities rarely go exactly as planned. New issues pop up, or any number of other things that can pull your meeting off course.

If you don't adjust to these events during the meeting, you could run out of time, fail to produce the output, and need to schedule another meeting. No one wants that. Being able to make adjustments on the fly is key to keeping things on track.

Adjusting your meeting doesn't have to be complicated. Here's how you can do it:

1. **Observe Changes in Direction:** Pay attention to where the conversation is going and be alert to large deviations away from the main purpose.

2. **Decide if a Deviation is Significant:** If a discussion seems off topic for more than a minute, it's time to step in.

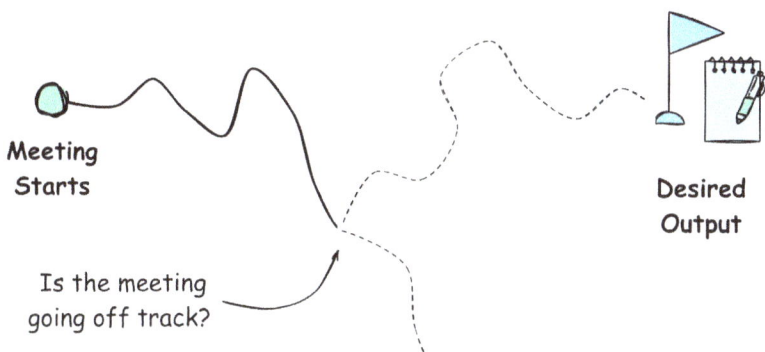

Meeting Starts

Is the meeting going off track?

Desired Output

3. **Choose How to Adjust:** If the conversation is too far off course, you have two options:

    o   **Option 1: Refocus the Discussion:** Bring it back to the original purpose. For example, "We seem to be getting sidetracked with topics not related to the project timeline. Let's refocus on our main objective."

    o   **Option 2: Change the Meeting's Goal:** Sometimes a new issue comes up that's more urgent than the original purpose and output. In this case, you may need to shift the meeting to something new. For instance, "It looks like we've uncovered a new issue that needs a solution before we can continue. Should we change the purpose of the meeting to focus on resolving this instead of our original goal?"

4. **Communicate the Adjustment:** If the decision is to change to a new purpose or output, make sure everyone understands.

5. **Continue the Meeting:** Whether you're heading back toward the original output or changing track, guide the conversation toward the desired output.

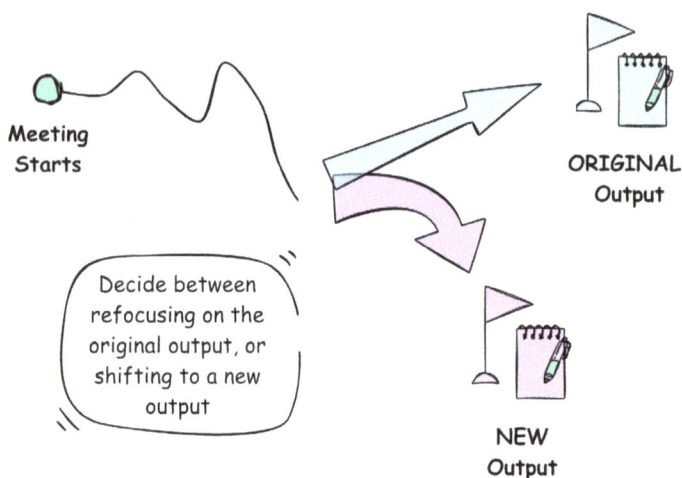

Meeting Starts

Decide between refocusing on the original output, or shifting to a new output

ORIGINAL Output

NEW Output

If there are multiple topics, repeat the process for each topic in the meeting. End each segment with a quick summary, clearly state any decisions or actions, and then move on to the next topic.

IMPORTANT: If the meeting changes direction to focus on a new output, you must decide what happens to the original purpose and output. Is it no longer needed? Do you set up a new meeting for it? Make a conscious choice so it's not forgotten!

Sometimes a conversation needs to move faster. The direction can be fine, but it's taking too long to get the work done. You'll notice this when keeping an eye on the clock shows the progress toward the output doesn't match the time that's passed. In these cases, you need to focus and speed up the conversation.

Phrases to Help Bring Things Back on Track

If you feel the meeting is drifting but you're not sure what to say, here are a few phrases you can use to pull it back on track:

» "It seems we're getting off track. Can we refocus on [original purpose + output]?"

- » "I'm a little lost. Can you remind me how this links to [original purpose + output]?"
- » "Sorry if I missed something, but I'm struggling to connect this to [original purpose + output]. Can you help clarify?"
- » "This seems important, but should we schedule a separate meeting for it so we can focus on [original output] here?"
- » "We're going into a lot of detail. Do we need this to achieve [output]?"

These phrases work no matter your role, whether you're leading the meeting or just attending. Asking questions is a great way to bring focus back without seeming rude. Just be mindful of your tone and timing to keep things respectful and constructive.

When Going Off Track is Valuable

You should try to keep meetings on track and always try to complete the output you set out to create. That being said, there are a few situations where letting the meeting go off track can be useful. If the purpose of the meeting is to do something creative, then twists, turns, and tangents are an important part of the process. In these cases, allow for more flexibility but still keep an eye on the overall time and progress to make sure you eventually reach your output.

If You're Not Leading the Meeting

The people leading meetings have an obvious responsibility for keeping things on track. But so do all the other participants. In fact, I'd argue that the participants have a bigger impact on the success or failure of a meeting than the leader. After all, there is only one leader, and they are outnumbered by the participants.

If you're a participant and notice things going off track, don't be afraid to speak up. A simple question can help refocus the group without stepping on the leader's toes. "I'm sorry if I missed something, but can someone help me see how the current topic relates to the output we are aiming for?" This way, you either learn why the current discussion is relevant or you help the meeting get back on track.

If we change our mindset from "meeting leaders are responsible for success" to "we are all responsible for the success of a meeting," the number of successful meetings goes up significantly.

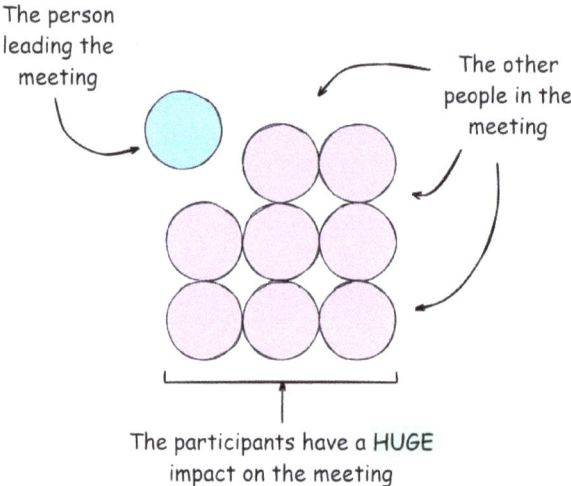

The person leading the meeting

The other people in the meeting

The participants have a HUGE impact on the meeting

INTERRUPTIONS AND DISRUPTIONS

Despite your best efforts to move at the right speed and keep things on track, there will be times when the other participants make it difficult. Some people won't stop talking, going into ever deeper levels of detail on their topic. Others try to disrupt or dominate the conversation, speaking over others and constantly interrupting. When faced with interruptions and disruptions, try the following methods to get the meeting back on track.

Some of the situations covered next, like "How do I handle disagreements and conflict?" have entire books written about them. I don't claim to give complete or perfect answers to those questions, but the methods described in the next few pages are a good place to start. They have helped me, and I am sure they will help you too.

Dealing With Repeated Interruptions

Some people just can't help themselves. They speak over people, interrupt, and try to take center stage. Whether the offender interrupts you or someone else in the meeting, here's how to handle it so it doesn't become an issue in your meetings:

1. **Intervene Early:** After the first few interruptions, set the tone. "Let's make sure everyone gets a chance to speak."

2. **Address it Directly:** Politely say, "Please let [speaker] finish their thought."

3. **Acknowledge and Redirect:** "I appreciate your enthusiasm, but let's hear [speaker] out first."

4. **Clarify the Reason:** "It seems like you have something urgent. Can it wait until [speaker] finishes?"

5. **Use Hand Signals:** If needed, implement a hand-raising system to control who speaks next.

6. **Follow-Up Privately:** If the behavior continues, talk to the person one-on-one after the meeting.

Interrupting Someone Without Being Rude

If someone is taking up time with long monologues and too much detail, you might need to be the person doing the interrupting. This can feel awkward, especially if it's your boss or a senior colleague. Here's how to do it without causing drama:

1. **Have a Reason:** Make sure there's a good reason to interrupt, like clarifying something, staying on topic, or managing time.

2. **Use Body Language:** Lean forward or raise your hand slightly to signal you want to speak.

3. **Be Polite:** Start with "Excuse me," or "I'm sorry to interrupt."

4. **Acknowledge Their Point:** Recognize what they were saying, like "I appreciate your insights, but to keep us on track…"

5. **Refer to the Meeting's Purpose:** Use the meeting's topic, purpose, and output as a reason for the interruption. For example, "To keep us on track with our goals today…"

6. **Ask a Question:** A good question can help redirect the conversation, like "How does this relate to our main goal today?"

Stop Someone Dominating the Conversation

Some people just love to talk, but it's important to make space for others. If there's a dominating voice in your meeting that's putting the purpose or output at risk, try these strategies:

» **Acknowledge and Redirect:** "Thanks for your input. Let's hear from others now."

» **Encourage Participation:** "Great points! Who else has thoughts on this?"

» **Summarize and Shift:** "I hear you saying [summary]. Let's get some other perspectives."

» **Set Time Limits:** "We appreciate your insights. To stay on track, let's hear from someone else."

» **Link to the Agenda:** "This is great info, but let's table it for now so we can focus on reaching [output]."

Managing a Disagreement or Conflict

When ideas or personalities collide, tempers can flare and quickly derail a meeting. There are so many causes for conflict and almost as many methods for handling it, to the extent that entire library shelves are filled with books on the topic. If you regularly face conflict in your meetings, you should investigate those books to find something that helps. But if conflict is rare, here are some general rules that will help resolve many meeting conflicts.

» **Stay Neutral:** Don't take sides. Let everyone share their views.

» **Encourage Respect:** Remind everyone to communicate respectfully.

» **Assess the Conflict's Relevance:** Is the disagreement helping or hurting the meeting's purpose?

» **Intervene:** Politely interrupt if the conflict is off track, using the techniques mentioned earlier.

» **Acknowledge and Redirect:** "Let's focus on what we agree on and find a solution that works for everyone."

» **Provide Structure:** Help each side summarize their points related to the meeting's goals.

» **Suggest Private Resolution:** If things escalate, suggest taking the disagreement offline.

When Participants Aren't Engaged

Not all disruptions involve people actively doing something. Sometimes it's the lack of action that causes a problem. It's hard to create an output if people aren't paying attention. People not being involved in the activities can cause as many problems as people being disruptive. If that happens, here are some options for what you can do:

» **Check for Monologues and Dominance:** Are one or two people dominating the discussion? Has one person been talking for five minutes nonstop? Is there a deep technical discussion happening with only some of the participants involved? If yes, this will cause everyone else to check out. Use the previous tips in this section to rebalance participation.

» **Directly Engage:** Take a direct approach to get people involved by asking non-engaged participants specific questions to draw them in.

» **Change the Activities:** When the activity is right, there should be energy in the room. If people aren't engaging, try switching to a different activity to involve everyone.

» **Ask for Feedback:** If lots of people seem disengaged, ask for feedback on how to improve.

Changing activities mid-meeting and asking for feedback can feel awkward, but that's better than continuing to run an unproductive meeting. I experienced this firsthand. During the second half of a ninety-minute meeting, I sensed the participants weren't engaged in an activity and asked them what could be done to improve it. One suggestion caught everyone's attention, and we changed the activity from a large group discussion to everyone working in pairs. The change immediately got everyone involved and we produced the desired output.

TAKE NOTES

The heading above says it all—*take notes*. I shouldn't need to say any more, but just to be sure you and I are thinking about the same thing, I'll expand a bit.

If you completed all the planning steps from chapter 1, you will already be prepared for someone to take notes. It could be you, a participant, or an automated tool like Fathom, Otter.ai, or CoPilot. What really matters is that *someone* is taking notes and you know who it is.

The second thing is to make sure the notes include the right things. The most useful meeting minutes and notes include a list of the decisions made, actions to be taken, questions to be answered, and the next step. This, coupled with the output, is all you need for meeting minutes. (Check out chapter 5 for examples of what the minutes and notes could look like.)

One thing you are unlikely to need is a complete word-for-word transcript of the entire meeting. Transcripts are great for witnesses in court, but Jessie from Accounts doesn't need, and won't read, a minute-by-minute account of the Monday morning team meeting. If for some reason you do need a complete record of what was said, record the meeting. It's more accurate than trying to type everything people say and easy to do with a mobile phone or by dialing into a video conference and recording it there.

How well do your meetings stay on track? Find out by using the simple assessment on the next page.

In a recent planning meeting, we made some crucial decisions, but no one took notes. Afterward, people had different recollections of what we'd agreed upon. We had to hold another meeting to clear up the confusion. No one was happy about that! What a waste of time.
—James, Product Owner

ASSESSMENT

HOW DO YOU RUN YOUR MEETINGS?

The quickest way to improve your meetings is to find the things your meetings are missing and focus on those. Take this quick assessment to find where to focus your attention in your meetings.

Think about the last few meetings you led and answer these questions:

» Did the meetings produce the desired outputs? If no, why not?

» If you ran the meetings again, would you keep the same activities?

» Did you actively look out for tangents and topics going off track?

» Did you actively track the progress toward creating the outputs?

» Did anyone take notes of the actions and decisions?

If you answered NO to anything, what was the impact on the meeting? What will you do differently to avoid it happening again?

CHAPTER 4

ENDING THE MEETING

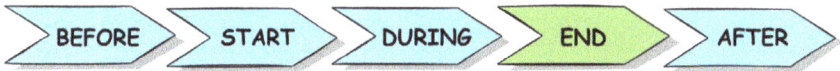

BEFORE > START > DURING > END > AFTER

How a meeting ends is just as important as how it starts. A bad ending can ruin even the best meeting. It is a sign of poor time management, makes the meeting feel incomplete, and it's frustrating. By contrast, a good meeting end reinforces what was achieved and sets the stage for what comes next.

By dedicating a small amount of time to a proper wrap-up and ensuring you finish on time, you leave participants with a positive impression and clear direction.

> *The worst sin is usually committed at the end of a meeting. The host says "anything else?" and then some moron brings up a topic that requires thirty more minutes of discussion.*
> **—Reddit user Anon8675309**

HAVE A FIVE-MINUTE WRAP-UP

We've all been in meetings that ran out of time. The leader realizes they're out of time, but the discussion is still going, so they interrupt and say, "Sorry, we're out of time. We'll have to continue this next time." This abrupt ending can cause the following unfortunate outcomes:

» **Unclear Actions:** People might not know what they're supposed to do or who's responsible.

» **Forgotten Decisions:** Decisions made during the meeting might not be remembered correctly, leading to mistakes.

» **A Poor Reputation:** Consistently ending meetings poorly makes you look like you can't manage time, which isn't great for your career.

To avoid these problems, set aside at least the last five minutes for a good wrap-up—longer if the meeting is more than an hour. Wrapping up properly ensures everyone leaves with a clear understanding of what was achieved and what needs to happen next.

Whatever happens, *protect* the wrap-up time. Don't give it away! I remember a great meeting that was going perfectly until the last few minutes. The team had nailed the output, and we had about ten minutes left—plenty of time for a wrap-up. But then someone asked an interesting question that wasn't directly related to the meeting purpose. The leader let the conversation run, and before we knew it, those ten minutes were gone. He tried to squeeze the wrap-up into the two remaining minutes. It was rushed but still overran the official end time, so everyone left feeling frustrated. What could've been a solid wrap-up turned into a scramble.

HOW TO CONDUCT A FIVE-MINUTE WRAP-UP

To have an effective wrap-up, follow these six steps:

1. **Allow Enough Time for the Wrap-Up:** Plan for it from the start. Don't let the discussion take up all the meeting time.

2. **Summarize the Meeting:** Quickly go over the key points discussed.

3. **Confirm Output Status:** Make sure everyone knows if the meeting's goal was achieved. Did you create the output or not?

4. **Recap Decisions and Actions:** Review any decisions made and actions to be taken. Be specific about who will do what by when.

5. **State Next Steps:** Outline what happens next at a high level, beyond just the individual actions. If the output wasn't completed, say what will happen next to make sure it is complete.

6. **Thank the Participants:** Acknowledge everyone's contributions and thank them for their time.

Remember, a wrap-up is a summary, not a detailed review. Make sure you use common sense to decide what level of detail is appropriate. If you achieved the meeting's goal, state that clearly. If you didn't, explain what still needs to be done.

Practical Example

Let's say you've led a meeting to finalize a proposal for an end-of-year event. Five minutes before the end, you start to wrap up. Here's what you could say:

» **Summarize the Meeting:** "Let's quickly recap. We were here to finalize the proposal for the end-of-year celebration, including decisions on the theme and whether to combine it with the annual awards."

» **Confirm Output Status:** "Our goal was to finish the proposal, and we did. We now have a document ready to share with the CEO and CFO for approval."

» **Recap Decisions and Actions:** "We decided to combine the awards ceremony with the end-of-year celebration in December. Claire will find volunteers to help with planning and setup, and Raj will send me the quotes from the event venue. I'll finalize the proposal today using the details from the quotes and this discussion. Is there anything I have missed or that needs correcting?"

» **State Next Steps:** "Great. The next step is that I'll send the proposal to the CEO and CFO tomorrow and then share their feedback with you all, probably by email. We each have our tasks, and I'll set up our next meeting for Thursday morning next week. The focus of that meeting will depend on the feedback we get, but I'll make sure the purpose is clear in the invite."

» **Thank the Participants:** "Thanks for your efforts today. We accomplished a lot and stayed on track, avoiding the need for a second meeting this week. Great job, everyone!"

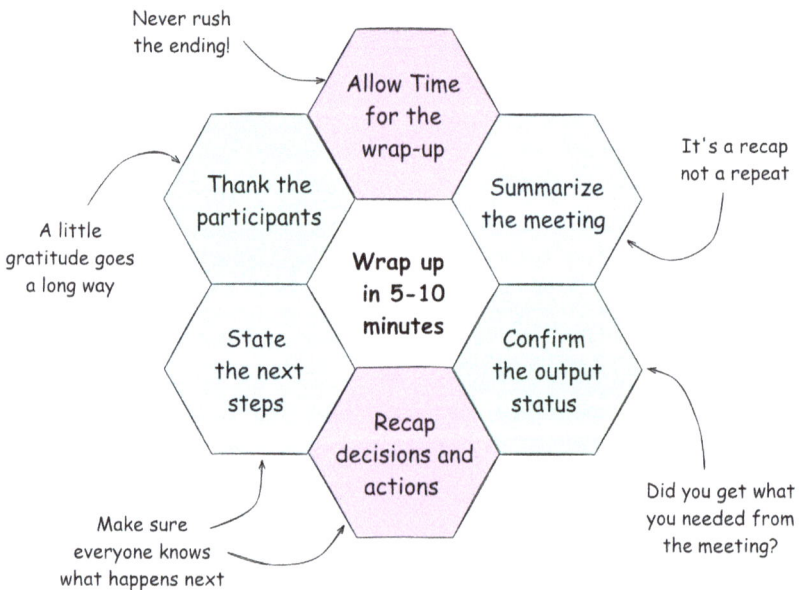

Never rush the ending!

Allow Time for the wrap-up

Thank the participants

Summarize the meeting

It's a recap not a repeat

A little gratitude goes a long way

Wrap up in 5-10 minutes

State the next steps

Confirm the output status

Recap decisions and actions

Make sure everyone knows what happens next

Did you get what you needed from the meeting?

Delivering this wrap-up should take about two to three minutes. In a more complex meeting, it could easily fill five minutes or more.

A proper wrap-up ensures everyone leaves the meeting with clarity and a sense of accomplishment. So, always save those last few minutes to bring everything together and end on a high note.

FINISH ON TIME

Finishing a meeting on time is simply the right thing to do. It shows respect for everyone's time and makes you look like a pro. Ending late, on the other hand, can leave a bad impression and throw off everyone's schedule. You know how frustrating it is when someone else's meeting runs over and makes you late. Don't be that person.

Running late doesn't just mess with your schedule, it affects everyone. Here's why you should aim to always end on time:

» **You Make Others Late:** If your meeting runs over, people will be late for whatever is next on their calendar.

» **Annoyance and Stress:** It frustrates everyone and creates unnecessary stress. Think about how you feel when you're late. When you make other people late, you are making them feel the same way.

» **Stealing Time:** You're taking more time than people agreed to give, and that's just not fair.

» **Reputation Damage:** Ending late shows you can't manage time well, which isn't great for your credibility.

» **Creates a Culture of Lateness:** If meetings consistently run over, it sets a precedent. Soon, everyone thinks it's okay to overrun.

» **Lose Your Complaining Rights:** Last but by no means least, if you end your meetings late, you lose the moral high ground. You are never allowed to complain about other people who start or end their meetings late.

Remember though, that finishing on time isn't just about ending when the clock strikes. Every part of the meeting contributes to a successful ending. It starts with your preparation. You need a clear purpose, the right people in the room, and the right activities to complete the output. During the meeting, you must stay focused on the goal, keep an eye on the clock, and leave room for a proper wrap-up. The final step? Actually finishing on time.

There's no magic trick to finishing on time. It comes down to good preparation and following the steps outlined so far in this book.

If time is running out but the discussion is still active, don't be afraid to interrupt. It might feel rude, but it's necessary to keep things on track. Try saying something like, "We've done as much as we can today. Let's start wrapping up so we can all leave on time." The mention of leaving on time should be enough to get most people to stop their discussions.

Here's the good news, finishing when you say you will shows you respect people's time. Participants are more likely to leave feeling good about what the meeting achieved as well as being more likely to attend future meetings you arrange.

Which is Better, Ending Late or Not Completing the Output?

There will be times when you have to choose between achieving the meeting purpose and finishing on time. This isn't a fun choice. On the one hand, you want to get the output, and on the other, you want to respect everyone's time.

If there is no way to complete the output and finish the meeting on time, I suggest you choose ending on time. It's the polite thing to do and sets the right precedence, inviting positivity instead of apprehension for the next meeting invite.

If the output is time-sensitive and absolutely must be finished right away, then ask the participants if they are able to stay. It's not ideal, but if they understand the importance of the work and are able to stay, you might avoid annoying anyone. Always ask—never assume that your meeting is more important than whatever else the participants have next on their schedule.

Whatever you do, make sure you don't fail on both accounts. Ending late and not completing the output is not good for anyone. How well do your meetings end? Find out by using the assessment on the next page.

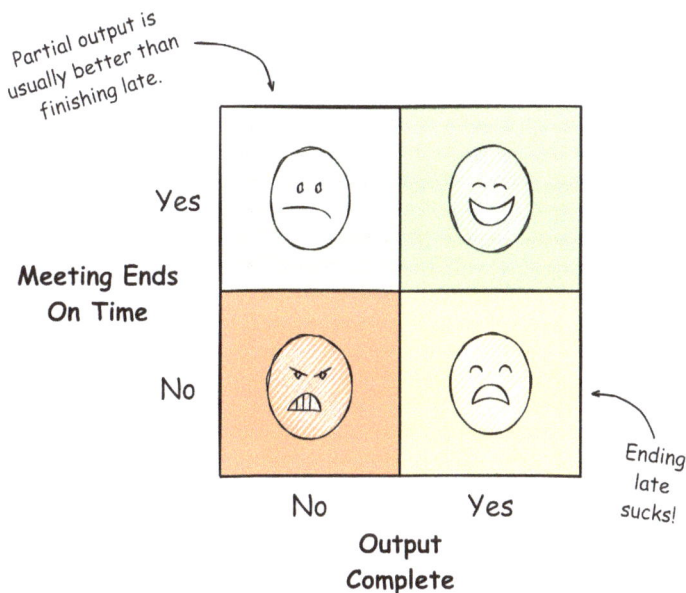

Partial output is usually better than finishing late.

Ending late sucks!

Meeting Ends On Time

Yes

No

No   Yes

Output Complete

> *Our weekly team meeting usually runs over by at least twenty minutes, so we're constantly late for our next meetings. Most of us have started blocking off half an hour after the meeting because we know it's going to overrun.*
> —**Leon, Customer Service Manager**

ASSESSMENT

HOW DO YOU END YOUR MEETINGS?

Do you consistently end your meetings well? Think of a recent meeting you led and answer these questions:

» How much time did you spend wrapping up the meeting?
» Was that enough time to give a good summary?
» Were the actions and decisions reviewed before the meeting ended?
» Did you clearly state the next steps?
» Did the meeting end on time?

If you answered NO to any question, what was the impact? What will you do differently in your next meeting?

CHAPTER 5

AFTER THE MEETING

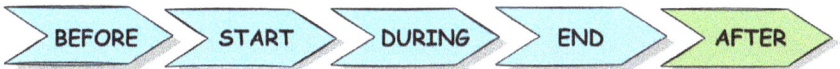

BEFORE > START > DURING > END > **AFTER**

Your work as a meeting organizer doesn't end when the meeting clock runs out. After the meeting you need to share the output and notes with the relevant people. Then, by diligently following up on actions and decisions, you reinforce the value of the meeting and help everyone maintain accountability.

In this part of the book, we will cover the two steps that should happen post-meeting.

1. Share the output and notes
2. Follow up on actions and next steps

By implementing these final steps, you will ensure all your efforts so far don't go to waste.

> *We had a design review to finalize requirements for a software up-date we needed to finish the next week. We worked for two hours and got loads done. I think we had forty or fifty changes to make to the product. Most were small things, but we knew it would be tight with only ten days left to make the deadline. But two days later there was still no sign of the list. It turned out the person taking the notes had gone on vacation! Seriously—you can't make this stuff up!!*
> —**Megan, Design Lead**

SHARE THE OUTPUT AND NOTES

It may seem obvious, but after the meeting ends you need to share the output with the relevant people. I've lost count of the times I had to ask someone to share the meeting output even when that output was clearly something many people needed to be able to do their daily work. There are two main reasons this step is crucial:

1. Every meeting should produce something—an action plan, a decision, a solution, etc. But that output is useless if it doesn't reach the people who need it. Plans need to be acted on, decisions need to be communicated, and ideas need to be tested.

2. If actions from the meeting aren't documented and shared, there's a good chance they won't get done or get done correctly, completely. People might forget all or part of their responsibilities without a clear record. Sharing notes boosts accountability and helps make sure things actually happen.

After your meeting ends, send the meeting's output and notes to everyone who needs them. This includes people who were in the meeting and those who weren't but still need to be kept in the loop about what was decided, what actions were assigned, and what's happening next. Do this as soon as possible, ideally within an hour of the meeting ending. This shouldn't take much time because the notes should be ready as soon as the meeting ends and just need some cleanup and formatting to make them more easily readable. There are a few rare exceptions when you might not need to share notes, like:

» When the meeting didn't produce an output and the only action is to set up another meeting.

» Celebratory meetings that don't have follow-up actions.

» Situations where the output was directly implemented during the meeting (e.g., a quick software fix).

» Secret meetings where no one wants a record (but let's not get into that).

How to Share the Output and Notes

When it comes to meeting notes, less is more. No one wants to sift through pages of notes. Here's what to include in your notes:

» **Finalize the Output:** Make sure the output is clear and easy to understand. If you made a list of ideas, tidy it up and format it nicely.

» **List of Topics Covered:** Provide a quick bullet-point list of the main topics discussed. Keep it simple, like: "Project updates, budget review, upcoming deadlines."

» **Include, Attach, or Link to the Output:** Make sure people have access to the actual output. This could be an attachment, a link, or just written out in the notes.

» **Questions and Actions:** Clearly list any actions assigned and any questions that still need answers.

   o Action: "John to finalize the budget by midday, June 5th."

   o Question: "Who will lead the marketing strategy?"

» **Decisions Made:** Note any decisions that were finalized in the meeting. If a decision still needs to be made, list it as an action.

   o Decision: "The project launch date is set for June 1st."

   o Action: "Derek to decide on the final launch date and email the team by 10 a.m. Wednesday."

Getting this step right keeps everyone informed and on track, including those who weren't able to attend the meeting. So, before you close your notebook or log off, make sure the right people get the right info so the work you did in the meeting doesn't go to waste and everyone knows exactly what to do next.

Practical Example

The next page shows an example of notes from a one-hour meeting. Without me giving you any extra information, you should be able to understand everything of relevance that happened in the meeting.

Hi everyone,

Here are the notes and output from the marketing plan review meeting today. Thank you for staying focused and getting everything done within the hour.

Next Steps: Please review the notes below, follow up on your tasks, and keep an eye out for an invitation to the next meeting. I'll send it this afternoon.

Jennifer,

» **Meeting Purpose:** Review the risk register for the current marketing plan and make sure it includes everything we need for the April and May promotions.

» **Outputs:** I'm pleased to say we completed everything in our target output. We now have a prioritized list of risks, decisions about how to manage each risk, and a list of tasks to ensure we deal with the biggest risks.

» **Risk Log:** The risk logs are up to date; access them here: [LINK]

» **Decision List:** The decision log was updated in the meeting; you can access it here [LINK].

- o The main decision we all need to remember is that the April promotion now has a limit on the number of discounted sales per customer and a maximum of three coupons per customer.

» **Tasks:** Most of us left with some tasks to do. Here is a list of who is doing what and when.

- o **Dave** will update the April coupon terms and conditions with the new limit of three sales per customer **by Thursday 11 a.m.**
- o **Sasha** will take the open questions to legal and share the answers with this group **by email tomorrow** (question list attached).

What Did You Do With The Notes & Output?

		Were they shared?	
		No	Yes
Were they created?	Yes	Unless it's a secret, send it out	Now that's what you call productive
	No	Why bother having the meeting?	I hope you have a good memory

FOLLOW UP ON ACTIONS AND NEXT STEPS

Next, you should follow up on the tasks, decisions, and questions that came up during the meeting to make sure things actually get done and the meeting's outcomes don't just fade away. A good follow-up keeps everyone on track and ensures the momentum from the meeting doesn't fizzle out. If no one follows through on what was discussed, then the meeting was pretty much pointless.

Here's what can go wrong if you skip the follow-up:

» **Unused Outputs:** The decisions or plans made in the meeting are forgotten or ignored, wasting the time used to create them in the meeting.

» **Unanswered Questions:** Any questions that came up but weren't answered fall through the cracks, leaving loose ends.

» **Shifting Priorities:** Without a reminder, people might shift their focus to other tasks, slowing down progress on the next steps.

» **Reduced Accountability:** If there's no follow-up, people are less likely to feel responsible for their tasks and important things might not get done.

» **Incomplete Actions:** Tasks might get missed entirely, which can stall progress.

It's not that people deliberately ignore what they need to do—there's just a lot competing for everyone's attention. A little follow-up can help keep things on track.

How to Follow Up

The way you follow up will depend on who you're dealing with or what was discussed. You probably wouldn't follow up with a senior executive the same way you would with someone in your team. No matter who you're following up with, here are some general tips:

» **Monitor Actions and Questions:** Keep track of the progress on tasks and make sure any pending questions get answered. Example: "John, have you had a chance to finalize the budget as we discussed?"

» **Send Reminders and Check-Ins:** Give people a gentle nudge to remind them of their tasks and offer help if needed. Example: "Hey, just a reminder that your tasks from [name the meeting] are due by the end of the day. Let me know if there's anything I can help with!"

» **Provide Updates:** Keep the relevant people updated on the status of follow-up actions and decisions. Example: "Just a quick update for the team—three out of five tasks are complete and the rest are on track for next week."

Unlike writing an invitation or leading a meeting, there isn't a one-size-fits-all example for following up. It really depends on your situation and the people involved. Use your best judgment and adapt your approach based on what will work best for your team. Remember, a little follow-up can go a long way in ensuring the meeting's outcomes are achieved and everyone stays accountable. Don't let the work done in the meeting go to waste—follow up to keep things moving forward.

ASSESSMENT

HOW DO YOU FOLLOW UP ON YOUR MEETINGS?

Think about the last meeting you led and answer these questions:

» Was the output shared with attendees after the meeting?

» Were the minutes shared with attendees after the meeting?

» How would you rate the overall quality of follow-up you did after the meeting? (Poor, okay, excellent?)

What would you do differently if you had to do the follow up again?

CHAPTER 6

TIPS FOR VIRTUAL
AND HYBRID MEETINGS

It doesn't matter if your meeting is in-person, virtual, or hybrid (a mix of both), as the advice in this book works for them all. But, online meetings have a few quirks you should be aware of. The following tips will help make your virtual meetings just as effective as those in person.

PAY ATTENTION TO THEIR ATTENTION

When you're in a room with people, it is pretty obvious if someone starts looking at their phone or using their laptop to write emails. Social pressure and a desire not to seem rude reduces the chance we would do anything like that, although I'm sure you've seen it happen. But, when we join a video call, the pressure to pay attention disappears. No one can see our computer screen or what's happening just outside the camera's view. And if we turn our cameras off, we have freedom to do whatever we want, safe in the knowledge that no one knows if we are paying attention or not.

When you run a hybrid or virtual meeting, you are fighting against dozens of distractions trying to get participants' attention. This puts extra importance on a clear and well-defined topic, purpose, and output. If people don't know what the meeting is for or how they are meant to contribute, they are more likely to give in to the temptations around them.

Keep a close eye on those little images of the participants. As tempting as it is to focus on the person speaking, or on your own image, you need to do the online equivalent of looking around the room. If you notice any participant's attention drifting, use the methods in chapter 4 to bring the focus back to the meeting.

USE ONLINE TOOLS TO YOUR ADVANTAGE

Virtual meetings have a lot of tools that can actually make things easier. You can use breakout rooms for small group discussions without the hassle of people physically moving around. Virtual whiteboards, polls, surveys, and shared documents make collaboration easier.

Get familiar with the way your company's online meeting tool works. Spend an hour learning how to set up and use things like polls and breakout rooms. The more familiar you are with what's possible, the easier it will be to use the tools to support your meeting.

LET THE PARTIAL PARTICIPANTS LEAVE

In chapter 3 I talked about managing multitopic meetings where some people are only needed for part of the meeting. Virtual meetings make it much easier to manage the partial participants. Letting them leave when their part is complete causes zero disruption to the meeting. There is no scraping of chairs or noisy movement. They just hit the exit button and leave. Just remember to wrap up properly at the end of their topic before letting them go.

WATCH OUT FOR MISSING VISUAL CUES

One big downside of virtual meetings is missing out on body language and facial expressions. In person, you can easily pick up on someone's frustration when they lean back, cross their arms, and sigh. Online, it's harder to catch these signals, especially if all you see is a head and shoulders—or worse, a blank screen if their camera is off. This makes it tougher to gauge how people are reacting, which can limit your ability to manage the flow of the meeting.

The easiest way to deal with this? Make "camera on" the rule. Seeing someone on camera, even if it's just their face, is a lot better than not seeing them at all. Sure, not everyone will love this, but think about it—when you're in a room with other people, you don't hide behind a curtain. Why should it be any different with virtual meetings? If people have their cameras off because they're multitasking or doing something else, they're not fully engaged and that's going to drag the meeting down.

Exceptions to the "Camera On" Rule:

There are a few reasons you may not want everyone to have their camera on. Consider allowing people to switch their camera off in the following situations:

» **Partial Participants:** If someone only needs to be there for part of the meeting, they can have their camera and mic off until it's their turn to participate.

» **Sensitive Locations:** Anyone working in an area where access is limited for security reasons.

» **Time-Zone Considerations:** If the meeting falls outside of regular working hours, especially late at night or very early in the morning and people are connecting from home.

» **Connection Issues:** You may also need to make allowances for people with a poor internet connection.

» **Religious or Cultural Observances:** During certain periods or observances, some may prefer to keep their cameras off due to cultural or religious practices.

By using the right tools and setting clear expectations, you can make sure your virtual meetings are just as productive and engaging as those held face-to-face.

TECHNICAL CHALLENGES

Nothing reduces the effectiveness of a meeting like technology problems. Online and hybrid meetings are plagued with issues like people unable to access the meeting, problems with the sound, or admin rights preventing the use of simple tools like screen sharing.

All sorts of issues make online meetings harder to run, but I am not going to go into detail on how to fix the issues here. There so many of them that this book could easily double in length. Not only that, the variety of meeting tools and the speed at which they change means anything I write here could be out of date before you pick up this book. Here I'll share with you how to avoid tech issues, generally speaking, so you can navigate this ever-changing landscape long term.

How to avoid tech issues with your meeting tools:

1. Get familiar with the meeting software your company uses. Spend time exploring its features, FAQs, and How-To information.

2. Find the troubleshooting guide for the most common issues for your software. Read it and keep it somewhere easy to access in case you need it in a meeting.

3. Do a technical test before an important meeting and periodically, especially after the software company rolls out updates.

That last point is a requirement for all my important online meetings. Before delivering workshops online, I spend 15-30 minutes online with the client testing the settings. This is to make sure I can access everything I need to run a good event with them. This has saved me multiple times when we discovered a simple feature was unexpectedly blocked by the way a company had set up the permissions on their video software.

DOUBLE CHECK YOUR ACTIVITIES

Chapter 1 described how to pick activities that support the meeting purpose and consider the limitations of people's locations. Whatever you do in the meeting should be equally accessible for all participants. The value of a voting poll is significantly reduced if four people in a room can only submit a single vote using the group laptop. If you have a group in a room and only a few are joining remotely, using sticky notes and flip charts on the walls to capture ideas will not work for the people online. Choose carefully and ensure everyone can take part and contribute.

ONLINE MEETINGS SHOULD BE SHORTER

Meetings should always be as short as possible, but online meetings should be even shorter. It takes more mental energy for participants to remain focused in an online meeting. It also takes more effort to run an online meeting and keep everyone engaged. If you think you need more than an hour for an online meeting, schedule breaks where people can get away from their screens for a few minutes. A good rule-of-thumb is to have a ten-minute break every hour.

CHAPTER 7

LESS PAINFUL STATUS UPDATE MEETINGS

STATUS UPDATING ... PLEASE WAIT

"Uuugghhh – do I have to do this?" That was my reaction when I realized I had to write this chapter. I don't like status update meetings—and I'm guessing you don't either. But they're an unavoidable part of work. Since we can't eliminate them, let's at least make them useful. The following pages will give you the tools to cut your status meetings in half, make them more effective and, I hope, less painful.

WHAT IS A STATUS UPDATE MEETING?

By "status update meeting," I mean the recurring sessions where people take turns sharing information about their work or the work of their teams. Most of this information is irrelevant to others in the room—making these meetings the soul-crushing, time-wasting kind that clog our calendars.

WHO ARE THEY FOR AND WHY DO THEY WANT THEM

The typical status update meeting exists because one person (a leader, project manager, or client) wants updates from multiple people at once. For that person, it's efficient—they hear everything in one go. But for everyone else, it's largely a waste. A well-structured written report could replace most of these. This is the classic "meeting that could have been an email."

WHY ARE STATUS UPDATE MEETINGS BROKEN

The core problem is lack of purpose. "Share the status of your work" is vague, so attendees guess what to include. They over-share to cover all bases, making the meeting longer. Others hide problems for fear of looking bad, or give excessive detail to 'prove' their worth. Either way, value drops for everyone.

HOW TO FIX YOUR STATUS MEETINGS

If you're thinking about having a status update meeting, you can greatly improve the chance of it being valuable by following these steps:

1. **Ask if a meeting is even needed.** If the only person who benefits from the update is you, don't have the meeting. Look for alternative ways to get information such as reports or 1:1 conversations.

2. **Define the purpose.** Decide what information is needed and how to best use everyone's time. Instead of "updates" you might want to focus on timeline reviews, issue discussions, risk planning, budget impacts, celebrating successes, etc. If it's just information sharing, find another method.

3. **Use a framework.** Instead of making people guess what you want to hear, tell them exactly what to cover. Structures and scripts like the two examples below help make updates relevant, clear, and, most importantly, short.

STRUCTURE FOR A STATUS UPDATE

1. **Introduce the update.** Start with a summary of the various topics in the update.

2. **Ask for the leader's priorities.** Ask what they want to hear about first. If you don't, they may be distracted or impatient, waiting for the topic they care about most.

3. **Update on what matters most to the people in the meeting.** Lead with updates that affect something the attendees care about—especially changes or impacts they need to know.

4. **Next, cover what you need from them.** Share topics where input, approval, or action is required.

SCRIPT FOR A STATUS UPDATE

Introduction:

» *"I have updates on these 3 things: [Topic 1], [Topic 2], [Topic 3].*

» *"Would you like to hear about anything else today?"*

Script for each update topic:

» *"For topic X I have an update that impacts [person | team | project | goal ABC]"*

» *"It is connected to [objective | goal XYZ]"*

» *"The problem is there is a change in the expected effort or outcome ... "*

» *"This impacts the [person | team | project | goal] in this way ... "*

» *"For the solution here's what I [need | think | want] to happen next ... "*

» *"Is there anything else you want to know about any part of this update?"*

The problem and impact don't need detail about what happened or why. Both can be quickly defined in terms of changes to the effort and outcome categories listed on the next page.

EFFORT	OUTCOMES
• Money	• Financial
• Time	• Speed
• Resources	• Efficiency
• Physical Energy	• Quality
• Mental Energy	• Compliance
	• Safety
	• Reputation
	• Satisfaction
	• Engagement

An extra benefit of using these effort and outcome categories to define the impact of your status update is that your message will be much clearer for the audience. Why? Because the expert language (jargon) is removed.

AFTER THE UPDATES

Plan to spend time on questions and discussion but be careful not to let discussions drift off track. It's tempting to solve problems as soon as they're raised, but that's rarely the meeting's main purpose. If the issue can be resolved in two minutes, handle it on the spot. If it's more complex, record it as an action for someone to coordinate outside the meeting. Yes, that might mean setting up another meeting, but it will ensure the current meeting achieves what it is supposed to.

A FEW MORE TIPS TO IMPROVE STATUS MEETING

» **Help people prepare.** Give clear examples of the type of information they should bring.

» **Collect and share topics and impacts in advance.** Ask participants to submit their topics and impacts before the meeting. This helps you plan the order of discussion and enables attendees to prepare.

» **Limit updates to three topics per person.** More than that? Schedule a separate meeting dedicated to those items.

» **Apply the inverse time rule.** The fewer people impacted by an update, the less time it gets.

» **Plan the order of updates.** Don't just go around the room. Start with items that affect everyone and have the biggest impact, then move to less critical topics.

» **Avoid deep dives.** If a topic takes more than two minutes to explain, or the solution discussion drags, stop and assign an action to resolve it outside the meeting (or repurpose the meeting—see Chapter 3).

» **Share successes.** It's not all bad news. Make sure you celebrate relevant wins—but keep it brief.

» **Cut "work done" lists.** If there's no impact on others and no request for the boss, there's no update. That information belongs in a report, not in the meeting.

.

CHAPTER 8

THE MEETING SWEET SPOT

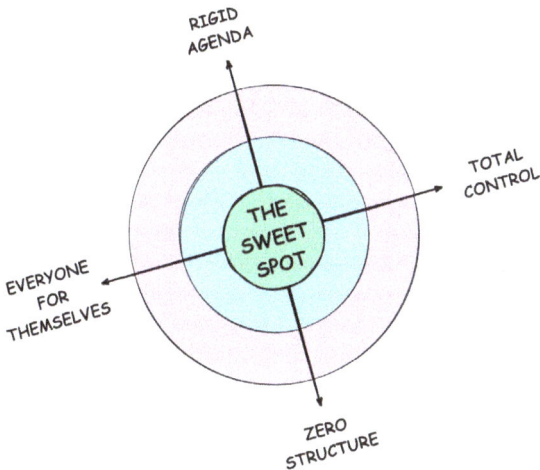

You are now equipped with the techniques to ensure your meetings will be shorter, more productive, and less frustrating. Nothing in this book is complex, but knowing the methods does not guarantee success. As with all tools, *how* you use them will define the success, or not, of your meetings. Not only that, but how you apply them will impact how other people think about you. Stick to the methods too rigidly, and you'll crush people's creativity and come across as controlling. Allow too much freedom for conversations to wander and fail to achieve the meeting purpose, and your people will think your meetings are a waste of time.

Meetings must have a clear agenda but be flexible, and the leader should stay in control but allow conversations to take unexpected paths. Talk about contradictory advice! The good news is you *can* do all these things—you can have an agenda and be flexible, stay focused and go with the flow. The secret is to find the balance between them. This is the meeting sweet spot.

As you become more comfortable using the methods described in this book, you'll find it easier to adapt them to different situations. There isn't one right way to lead a meeting. Different situations call for different levels of flexibility and structure. For example, a fifteen-minute daily standup meeting among software developers requires a different approach compared to a status update for the senior leadership team. Consider each meeting and pick the right level of structure, formality, and activity for the situation, audience, and purpose.

But beware! Flexibility is good until you move too far away from the sweet spot, and the result is bad. Very bad. Not only will the meeting fail to deliver what's needed but those operating too far from the sweet spot will quickly gain a name for themselves—and it may not be a name they like. The level of structure and control you use, or don't use, will influence which of the four types of bad meeting leader you could become.

1. **Tyrant** – Dominates the meeting with strict control over every part of the agenda and conversation. Alternative views are not welcome here.

2. **Chaotic Dictator** – Insists on making all decisions and maintaining control but lacks the structure or organization to do it effectively.

3. **Passive Enforcer** – Expects the group to stick to the plan but won't actively lead or control the discussion.

4. **Lord of Chaos** – Provides no structure or guidance, allows meetings to drift without direction or purpose and participants are left to fend for themselves.

WHAT TYPE OF MEETING LEADER ARE YOU?

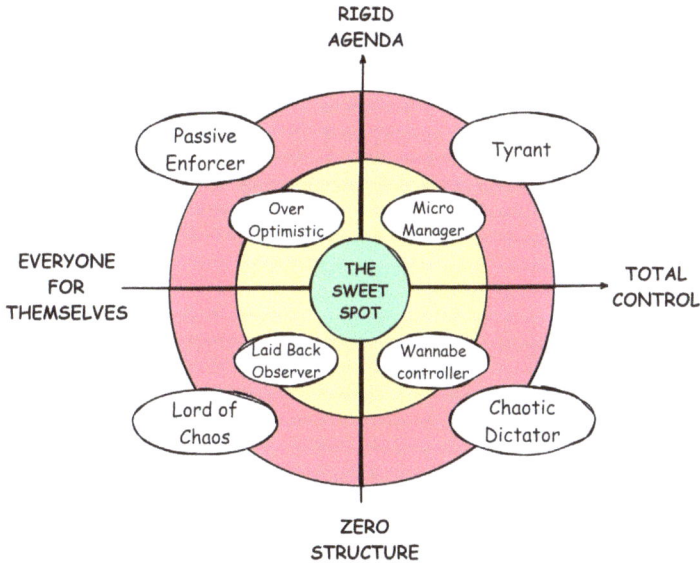

RIGID
AGENDA

Passive
Enforcer

Tyrant

Over
Optimistic

Micro
Manager

EVERYONE
FOR
THEMSELVES

THE
SWEET
SPOT

TOTAL
CONTROL

Laid Back
Observer

Wannabe
controller

Lord of
Chaos

Chaotic
Dictator

ZERO
STRUCTURE

These four leader types are the extremes. It's rare to find people with these labels, but they do exist, achieved when someone goes too far from the sweet spot. Most bad meeting leaders are less extreme but do maintain some of the less than ideal traits. These people fall into the following categories:

» **Overoptimistic**: Not as hands off as the Passive Enforcer but still has too much hope that people will manage themselves.

» **Micromanager**: Less dominant than the tyrant and more willing to hear other people's opinions, this leader still insists on controlling every part of the meeting.

» **Wannabe Controller:** This leader has a bit more organizational ability than the Chaotic Dictator but still isn't effective.

» **Laid Back Observer:** Moderately better organized and a little stricter than the Lord of Chaos, this leader still lets things run free even if it puts the meeting goals at risk.

The point of this isn't to label everyone as some form of a bad meeting leader. The goal is to help you see where you might sit on this scale to give you an idea of how you might adapt your style and find your own sweet spot.

This chart helped me improve my own style when leading meetings. My natural tendency sits somewhere between micromanager and overoptimistic, and it takes effort for me to counter these tendencies. But when I do, the results are always worth the effort.

What type of meeting leader are you? Are you always in the sweet spot? Or where do you fall in the ranges of leader types described above? Wherever you sit on this scale, think about how you want to show up.

Different meetings need different styles, and knowing your own style will help you adapt. Remember too, there is no one-size-fits-all approach. It's okay to deviate from the agenda if it supports the meeting purpose. Embrace the twists and turns of a conversation and you'll discover new things. Guide the discussion to stay focused on what's important but don't control every detail. And above all, as the meeting leader, your primary role is to help everyone stay on track and be successful in achieving the meeting's purpose. Stay flexible and you will find the sweet spot for each meeting you lead.

APPENDIX

THE ESSENTIAL ELEMENTS OF A GREAT MEETING

Sneakily hidden in the pages of this book are seventeen essential elements every great meeting needs. To make it as easy as possible for you to remember and apply all the elements of a productive meeting, here they are all in one place. You can also download a printable version from www.chrisfenning.com/resources.

BEFORE THE MEETING

1. **Do You Really Need the Meeting?** Before you begin planning, check if a meeting is the right way to get the work done.

2. **Define the Topic, Purpose, and Output:** Start with a clear understanding of what your meeting is about and what you aim to achieve.

3. **Pick the Activities:** Select activities that support your meeting's purpose and keep participants engaged.

4. **Choose the Right People:** Ensure everyone in the room has a reason to be there and can contribute to the meeting's goals.

5. **Pick the Location:** Whether in person, online, or a mix of both, the location should be accessible to everyone and a good fit for the necessary activities.

6. **Write a Great Invitation:** Communicate the meeting's details clearly to set expectations and prepare participants.

STARTING THE MEETING

7. **Introduce Your Meeting:** Begin by restating the topic, purpose, and output to align everyone from the start.

8. **Validate with the Participants:** Confirm that everyone understands and agrees on the meeting's objectives.

DURING THE MEETING

9. **Stay Focused on the Purpose and the Output:** Keep the discussion on track to avoid wasted time and off-topic conversations.

10. **Track Progress Against Time:** Monitor the time and ensure the meeting progresses toward its goals.

11. **Adjust Your Meeting to Stay on Track:** Be flexible and ready to steer the meeting back on course when necessary.

12. **Give Time Updates:** Keep participants aware of the time to maintain focus and productivity.

13. **Handle Multiple Topics:** For multitopic meetings, apply steps seven through twelve to each topic.

ENDING THE MEETING

14. **Have a Five-Minute Wrap-Up:** Reserve time at the end to summarize and confirm next steps.

15. **Finish on Time:** Respect participants' schedules by ending your meetings as planned.

AFTER THE MEETING

16. **Share the Output and Notes:** Distribute the meeting's outcomes, action items, and any important notes to all relevant parties.

17. **Follow Up on Actions and Next Steps:** Ensure that the work continues and all agreed-upon actions are completed.

RECOMMENDED READING

In the course of writing this book I reviewed a *lot* of books about meetings. Here are some that I think you'll like.

GENERAL BOOKS ABOUT MEETINGS

» *Hold Successful Meetings* by Caterina Kostoula. This book is a good guide for running problem-solving meetings, in addition to having lots of good advice about meetings in general.

» *Let's Stop Meeting Like This: Tools to Save Time and Get More Done* by Dick and Emily Axelrod. If your meetings focus on making big decisions or are helping connect people to the work they are doing, this is a great book.

» *Mission Critical Meetings: 81 Practical Facilitation Techniques* by Ava S. Butler. Are you looking for an activity or technique to help your meeting achieve its purpose? Then look no further than this book. It's a big book and has a lot of practical methods to choose from.

VIRTUAL MEETINGS

» *75+ Team Building Activities for Remote Teams: Simple Ways to Build Trust, Strengthen Communications, and Laugh Together from Afar* by Christopher Littlefield. While not fully focused on meetings, many of the seventy-five activities help make your remote meetings and one-on-ones more engaging.

» *Break Out of Boredom: Low-Tech Solutions for Highly Engaging Zoom Events by* Robbie Samuels. While focusing on Zoom, this book applies to any virtual meeting platform. It was written to support meeting professionals, virtual presenters, and virtual facilitators committed to hosting virtual meetings and conferences.

WORKSHOPS

Here are some of my favorite books about creating and running successful workshops. I have used them all to make my own training better.

» *The 2-Hour Workshop Blueprint: Design Fast. Deliver Strong. Without Stress* by Leanne Hughes. If you need to teach, engage, and entertain a room of strangers, this book will help you do a great job.

» *The Workshop Survival Guide: How to Design & Teach Workshops That Work Every Time* by Rob Fitzpatrick and Devin Hunt. From planning the content to handling troublesome attendees, this book is about as practical as they come.

» *Lead Engaging Meetings: A Practical Guide to Maximize Participation and Effectiveness* by Jeff Shannon. Despite what the title may imply, this book focuses on large half, whole, or multi-day events. If you're running a large event, this is a great guide.

And of course, if you want to make sure the training delivered in a workshop isn't forgotten, check out my award-winning book, *39 Ways to Make Training Stick: What to Do After Trainees Leave the Room.*

FOR BUSINESSES AND OTHER ORGANIZATIONS

If you want to improve meeting productivity in your organisation why not try one (or both!) of the following things:

1. Give your employees this book.
2. Have an engaging and interactive workshop with me.

Workshops are available virtually and in person and special rates are available for bulk book orders. You can even have your company logo added to the cover along with a message for your employees added to the introduction.

To find out more, send an email to chris@chrisfenning.com

ACKNOWLEDGMENTS

No book is created in isolation, and I am very lucky to have a group of dedicated and generous people to ensure the book you are reading is the very best it can be.

As always, Debra L. Hartmann, thank you for taking my words and molding them into something readable. How you put up with my terrible grammar I do not know, but I am certainly grateful. This is our third book together, and I look forward to working with you on many more in the future.

Danielle, you support me every day and have possibly the hardest job of all—you put up with my grumbling as I work through the frustrations of creating a book. As much as I'd like to promise it'll be easier next time, I know better than to tell such an obvious lie. I love you.

A huge thank you must go to the generous people who reviewed the book during the writing process. The final book is so far removed from the first version that it is almost unrecognizable. That is all your fault(!) and I'm very grateful for your honesty. You didn't pull your punches, you told me what I needed to hear, and the final result is so much better because of it.

Everyone who reads this book should be grateful to you: Renaud Taburiaux, Jensen Chiu, Ewa Hutmacher, Ignacio Ahedo, Yegor Korovin, David Sims, Yasmina Khelifi, David Sims, and Diane Bergman. Thank you.

Lastly, I want to thank the thousands of people who contributed to and those who suffered in the meetings I led throughout my career. You all helped shape the advice in this book.

DON'T MISS OUT!

Get your FREE copy of the
Effective Meetings resource kit.

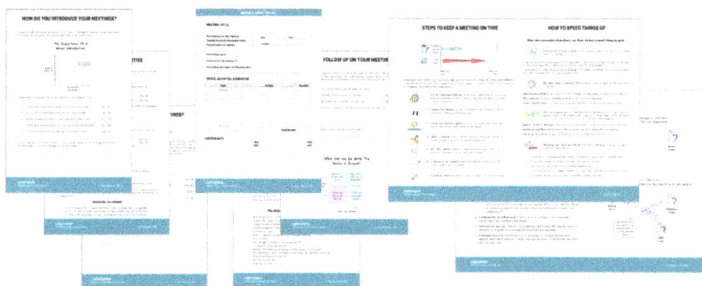

Get a free resource kit packed with assessments, guides, activities, templates, and examples. It will help you apply what you learn in this book to the meetings you have every week at work.

https://chrisfenning.com/resources/

www.ingramcontent.com/pod-product-compliance
Lightning Source LLC
Chambersburg PA
CBHW040928210326
41597CB00030B/5221